Food

FOOD LOVERS'
GUIDE TO
TAMPA BAY

The Best Restaurants, Markets & Local Culinary Offerings

1st Edition

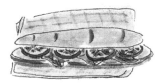

Todd Sturtz

Guilford, Connecticut

Editor: Amy Lyons
Project Editor: Lauren Brancato
Layout Artist: Mary Ballachino
Text Design: Sheryl Kober
Illustrations by Jill Butler with additional art by Carleen Moira Powell and MaryAnn Dubé
Map: Melissa Baker © Morris Book Publishing, LLC

ISBN 978-0-7627-8120-1

Printed in the United States of America

10 9 8 7 6 5 4 3 2 1

All the information in this guidebook is subject to change. We recommend that you call ahead to obtain current information before traveling.

Contents

Recipes, 215

About the Author

Todd Sturtz is not a funny guy, but oh how he tries. An engineer by education and a food lover by obsession, Todd became fascinated with food during college and spent what little "disposable income" he had on exploring new restaurants and cuisines in the years to follow. Todd soon took up cooking courses, obsessive-compulsive viewing of food-related TV programming, befriending as many local chefs as possible, even planning to open a restaurant and later talking himself out of it—all in the same two weeks! Quite likely Todd's greatest asset is his wife, Shannon, who not only has put up with all his shenanigans all these years but also had the fantastic disposition of growing quickly from a "meat-n-potatoes" girl into a more adventurous food-sharing companion than he could have hoped for. Todd started Tasting Tampa (TastingTampa.com) as a blog to connect good people with good food, and it quickly grew to be much more. Follow him at facebook.com/TastingTampa or on Twitter at @TastingTampa.

To my darling wife, who would likely never forget it
if I dedicated this book to anyone else.
(But seriously though, she's pretty awesome.)

Acknowledgments

I'd like to thank coffee. To my wife, Shannon, who has been willing on more than one occasion to eat at 30-plus restaurants in a weekend "R&D" trip to Manhattan without complaint, you are the most amazing person I've ever met. Don't change a bit. Thank you and much love to my parents for introducing me to good food and taking me with them on trips around the world when they could've just as easily left their annoying, complaining child at home. I'd like to thank Alton Brown and Anthony Bourdain for motivating my adventures in the kitchen and abroad; my food-modus-operandi is very much a mixture of their personalities. I suppose I should thank the people on Facebook who didn't un-friend me when I started relentlessly posting pictures of delicious-looking food and checking in at restaurants with reckless abandon—you guys are the best! I'd like to thank Bill, Cass, and Kurt, people I am proud to call friends whom I never would've met had it not been for our mutual love of food. I really appreciate everything you all introduced me to, shared with me, and the experienced knowledge you imparted with each enjoyable meal. A special thanks to Jeff Houck for being an inspiration when it comes to food writing and for believing in me. If there's anything I've been blessed with, it's a great family and great friends, and I could not possibly be more grateful.

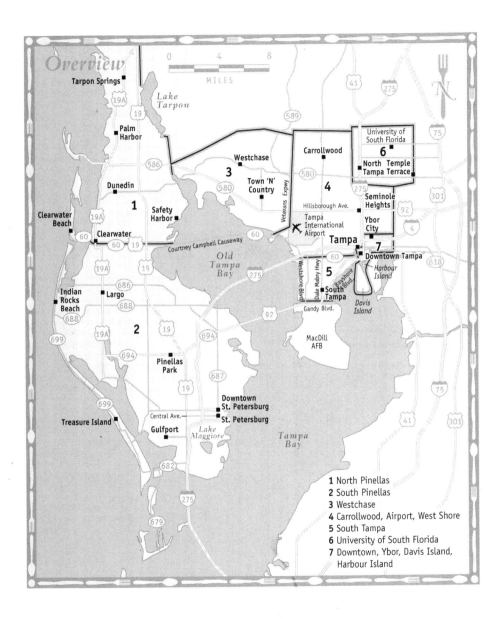

Overview

MILES
0   4   8

Tarpon Springs

Lake Tarpon

Palm Harbor

Westchase

Carrollwood

University of South Florida

6

North Temple Tampa Terrace

Dunedin

3

Town 'N' Country

Seminole Heights

Clearwater Beach

1

Safety Harbor

Hillsborough Ave.

4

Ybor City

Clearwater

Courtney Campbell Causeway

Tampa International Airport

Tampa

7

Downtown Tampa

Old Tampa Bay

Veterans Expwy

Harbour Island

Indian Rocks Beach

Largo

Westshore Blvd.

Dale Mabry Hwy.

5

South Tampa

Bayshore Blvd.

Davis Island

Gandy Blvd.

2

MacDill AFB

Pinellas Park

Downtown St. Petersburg

Central Ave.

St. Petersburg

Treasure Island

Gulfport

Lake Maggiore

Tampa Bay

N

1 North Pinellas
2 South Pinellas
3 Westchase
4 Carrollwood, Airport, West Shore
5 South Tampa
6 University of South Florida
7 Downtown, Ybor, Davis Island,
   Harbour Island

Introduction: Tampa—The Other "West Coast"

Welcome. If you're visiting Tampa, a new resident, or even a native born and raised, we're happy to have you. Enjoy our beautiful beaches, our scenic parks and architecture, our classic and preserved homes, great shopping, world champion sports teams, and best of all—our food! As an eighth-generation Floridian, a die-hard food lover, and a frequent traveler, I can assure you that you're in for a treat when it comes to the epicurean delights that fill the Tampa Bay area. I still recall with great clarity the first moment I really fell in love with food in Tampa, sitting solo at what instantaneously became one of my favorite restaurants of all time, Pane Rustica, biting into a sandwich so subtly simple yet beautifully complex (their play on an oyster po'boy). Time slowed down and things became quiet. My eyes focused on the cross-section of the sandwich, analyzing each component on a near-molecular level for just enough time to finish savoring the bite I had in my mouth and then inhaling the rest of it. House-baked olive loaf, thick sliced and pan toasted with a bit of olive oil, wrapped around plump tender oysters fried perfectly crispy and accented by a spicy house aioli and a few shreds of greens (for nutritional value, I'm sure). A brief trip to the kitchen to sing praises to the kind gentleman who made my sandwich (who had a bit of a bewildered look that I was in the kitchen, singing), and I drove back to the office, love-struck. I was never the same. Tampa has much more impressive food to offer than it often gets credit for. Please disregard entirely that our humble city has been the birthplace of many awful national chain restaurants, and focus on the restaurants in this book that support the area's farms and farmers, brewers, coffee roasters, and more.

Pull up a chair, munch on some nice Cuban toast with a *cafe con leche*, and I'll share with you a taste of the best we have to offer.

How to Use this Book

Tampa is not what most would consider a walking city (better than half the year, the climate is not conducive to it); few if any cities in Florida are. That isn't to say walking is out, traveling first via vehicle to Downtown Tampa or St. Petersburg, Tarpon Springs, Dunedin, and other neighboring areas makes for very fun pedestrian exploration, but as a primary means of transportation cars are king. Bearing that in mind (and bearing in mind the author is an engineer), the regions of Tampa Bay have been divided up more so by traveling paths than by neighborhoods—an atypical approach, but all the same great restaurants are still there for the picking.

The organization of this book is based primarily off the neighborhoods in geographical locations in the Tampa Bay area. There are three bridges connecting Hillsborough County (Tampa) to Pinellas County (Clearwater, St. Petersburg), and all serve for locals as more than just physical boundaries; they are in many ways mental boundaries, too. Residents of either county tend to eat in proximity to their respective locations (work, home, etc.) because crossing the bridge is a "commitment" that adds 20 or more minutes to any dining adventure. Pinellas County is approximately 35 miles long, with Hwy. 60 as one of the major east-west corridors running nearly directly through the middle of it, and people not centrally located to Hwy. 60 are much less likely to venture from North Pinellas County to South, and vice-versa.

Tampa is not as cleanly delineated. When asking where to eat, the question is most commonly prefaced with "that isn't far from the airport" or "that is near downtown" or "that is a short taxi ride from Ybor," etc. Some of Tampa's neighborhoods have been or are in a state of flux with regard to being "up and coming" or in a state of gentrification. Given that Tampa isn't really a walking city and most readers will be traveling by vehicle, the organizational structure of this book is such that restaurants in Hillsborough County are laid out in a more north-central-south-east-west format.

Foodie Faves

Foodie Faves encompasses restaurants new and old, staples and trends, and neighborhood favorites. Eateries in this category may be as inexpensive as a taco stand or as pricey as a multi-course prix fixe by candlelight.

Landmarks

This category of restaurants typically defines a decades-old classic restaurant with a rich history and a personality, but it may also refer to a more recent restaurant that has made such a strong impact on the local dining scene that it quickly became definitive thereof.

Specialty Stores, Markets & Producers

Tampa has hundreds of places to get coffee, bagels, baked goods, pastas, chocolates, cheeses, and more, but it has only a handful of places to do so that are truly fantastic. This section highlights spots that have made a notable contribution to the artisan goods scene in the Bay.

Price Codes

Given that price codes are difficult to convey without some gray area, the scale below takes into account a meal with an adult beverage, and that at a less-expensive restaurant diners might only be purchasing a plate of food and a beer, while at a fine-dining establishment wine or cocktails are probably the beverages of choice and the meal may include multiple courses. For non-drinkers, a meal will naturally be less expensive.

$ Meal typically under $15

$$ Meal typically $15 to $30 per person

$$$ Meal typically $30 to $60 per person

$$$$ Meal typically $60+ per person

Keeping Up with Food News

Staying on top of trending foods, hip and new restaurants, food events, and all other things tasty is most easily accomplished with a few keystrokes on the web, or by picking up an issue of one of our free food-friendly local publications at your favorite coffee shop.

Food Blogs

Carlos Eats (carloseats.com). A student, amateur photographer, blogger, and food lover, Carlos eats his way around the city, documenting his finds and sharing them with the community. A genuinely nice guy with a lot of energy and enough free time to really make his way all around town, Carlos is a good guy to follow if you're looking for a hidden gem or hole-in-the-wall that has excellent food you'd never have heard of otherwise.

The Stew—A Food Blog by Jeff Houck (tinyurl.com/ thestew). Jeff Houck is practically Tampa's food ambassador. He is the *Tampa Tribune*'s food writer, and his love for all things delicious is refreshing and heartfelt. Jeff's writing style is typically positive and critical only when warranted, an outlook that has garnered him many a fan both of his print articles and of his blog The Stew. Creator of the "Underbelly Tour" (Google it), Houck has taken local chefs and food lovers on nose-to-tail adventures through expensive and excitingly authentic ethnic res- taurants throughout the Bay to explore what the typical American palate often misses. Check out The Stew on Facebook or TBOBlogs.com.

Taylor Eason (tayloreason.com). Wine ninja and food aficio- nado Taylor Eason spent years in Tampa educating Floridians to love the subtle nuance of fermented grape juice and the food that complements it so well, until she was offered a fantastic job in California wine country. Few wine lovers in their right mind would pass up an opportunity like that, so rather than leave Tampa writing behind, Taylor passed the torch on to her friend Mary, who still writes the Tampa blog posts to this day.

Tasting Tampa (tastingtampa.com). Pretty much the best blog ever. Well . . . pretty much.

Local Publications

Creative Loafing (cltampa.com). Another free local arts and entertainment newspaper, Atlanta-based *Creative Loafing* has numerous contributing food columnists (including this book's author) and seeks out tasty grub at all price points all over the Bay.

The Local Dirt (localdirttampabay.com). Chef Ferrell Alvarez and business partner Ty Rodriguez (of Cafe Dufrain) created a free local magazine with the intent of moving the "Eat Local" culture in the Tampa Bay area forward, and they have caught the attention of many. *The Local Dirt* highlights local farms and farmers that grow high-quality produce without the use of genetic modification or unhealthy pesticides and ethically raise animals that are naturally fed hormone-free food. Also showcased in the magazine are restaurants and chefs that support these farms and farmers, as well as guides to buying local, a very honorable movement that is quickly picking up momentum in the Tampa Bay area.

TBT (tampabay.com/tbt). A sister publication to the newspaper the *Tampa Bay Times* (formerly the *St. Petersburg Times*) gauged toward a younger demographic, TBT is a free newspaper that focuses on arts and entertainment with food writers that seek out everything from fun, new, and trendy restaurants, to classics and Tampa institutions.

Food Websites

Chowhound (chowhound.chow.com/boards/10). Chowhound is a regionally subdivided community forum for discussing restaurants, recipes, and other foodstuffs in a given area. Look for recommendations and responses from frequent contributors, and be wary of any user being hypercritical or overly excited about a meal—they may be genuine in their commentary, but they also may be owners of a restaurant trying to put unearned praise for their own restaurant on the Internet.

Foodspotting (foodspotting.com). One refreshing aspect of the foodie website Foodspotting is that it is less opinion-based and features user-submitted pictures of food from restaurants in a specified area, so reading lengthy reviews is unnecessary—if the photo looks killer, the dish probably is!

Urbanspoon (urbanspoon.com/c/30/Tampa-Bay-restaurants .html). Urbanspoon is an international website that allows users to leave reviews and a "like" or "dislike" rating, showing the percentage of likes vs. dislikes for each restaurant on the restaurant's individual sub-page. This site functions as a decent guideline, but people often criticize with very biased intent (nothing prevents a restaurant owner from giving himself a sterling review and giving the competition a terrible one), so take everything with a grain of salt and don't trust any reviews from users who have only ever contributed a single review (usually they are owners or employees of the restaurant).

South Tampa

South Tampa is generally considered the peninsula south of Kennedy Boulevard (Hwy. 60) stretching south to Gandy Boulevard. It is one of the most affluent areas in the city of Tampa and is home to athletes, celebrities, and the like. Some neighborhoods in South Tampa date to the early 1900s, with many classic preserved homes, and real estate is anything but cheap. Given the density of disposable income, many restaurateurs have targeted the area to set up higher-end eateries, and many have become very successful doing so. Residents of South Tampa are often teased for never wanting to go NOK (North of Kennedy) or SOG (South of Gandy), but with a plethora of great restaurants to choose from along with beautiful homes and scenery (Bayshore Boulevard lines the eastern side of the peninsula and has the longest uninterrupted waterfront sidewalk in the USA), they don't need to!

Bianchi's Enoteca, 3215 S. MacDill Ave., Tampa, FL 33629; (813) 837-2233; bianchisenoteca.com; Italian/Wine Bar; $$$. Bianchi's Enoteca is a hidden gem of a wine bar close to a number of other great restaurants on South MacDill; blink and you may miss it! Two former employees of one of South Tampa's best-known wine shops joined forces and created a simple yet delightful menu of wines, cheeses, charcuterie, and small plates, and they quickly gained a loyal following. House-made country pâté, duck confit white bean salad, and anchovy bruschetta are just a few of the specialties that can be found at Bianchi's, along with a variety of wines by the glass or bottle, at a very approachable range of prices. Bianchi's decor parallels the menu: simple, small, and elegant. The space would be perfect for a small party and is often used for such.

BJ's Alabama BBQ, 3307 S. Dale Mabry Hwy., Tampa, FL 33629; (813) 374-0219; Barbecue; $. From the outside, BJ's Alabama BBQ isn't much to look at. From the inside, BJ's Alabama BBQ isn't much to look at. Step within a 50-foot radius and breathe through your nose though, and I'd wager you'll get pretty hungry. Just the smoky meaty smell emanating from this little barbecue gem is enough to get most people in the door, and the flavorful, rich, well-seasoned 'cue that they heap on your plate is enough to keep most people coming back for more. Typical of a barbecue joint, the menu is pretty simple with ribs, chicken, pork, and sides like baked beans, collards, mac n' cheese, and corn. The beauty is in the simplicity though, and the comforting smokiness and umami are good to the last bite.

Boca, 901 W. Platt St., Tampa, FL 33604; (813) 254-7070; bocatampa.com; American; $$$. Eat local. These two words carry more weight than many people understand, as buying food from local farms (rather than huge mass producers) not only supports local small business owners and contributes to the community but is also excellent for your health! Boca is one of the first restaurants in Tampa to fully focus a concept around supporting sustainable and fresh ingredients that are in season and sourced locally, and correspondingly they quickly garnered much attention. The building that houses Boca was actually built as a gas station over 80 years ago, and has since been a number of other businesses, but it retains a kind of interesting, retro design. The retro theme carries over a bit into the decor of the restaurant, with classic-looking music posters on the walls and various other throwback items strewn about. The front of the house is a bar looking into the kitchen, which can be a fun show to watch when things get busy, and the restaurant also offers a small market to purchase artisan goods, many of which are produced in Florida. Although only a few months old at the time this was written, Boca has already brought a lot of much-needed attention to the Eat Local movement in Tampa, and hopefully many more restaurants will continue to do so.

BT, 2507 S. MacDill Ave., Tampa, FL 33629; (813) 258-1916; restaurantbt.com; French/Vietnamese; $$$$. On South MacDill Avenue, where many a local-owned restaurant and boutique store exists, BT Nguyen set up shop with her new and refined French-Vietnamese fare. Previously, Restaurant BT occupied a much larger space in Hyde Park Village, but as with many businesses in that area, the recession became the eventual end of a beautiful thing. A testament to BT's spark and her vigor, she quickly rose like a phoenix from the ashes into a much more reasonably sized space and with even more beautiful decor than before. Sleek bamboo tables and completely transparent acrylic chairs hover over natural tile floors, while pieces of driftwood act as modern art on the walls and various artificial shrub arrangements very tactfully give the space a splash of color and life. The service is among Tampa's finest; classically French-trained servers delicately and politely do their best to assure your dining experience lacks nothing. The menu is equally elegant, with many dishes rooted in classic Vietnamese cuisine only to be elevated to a new level via infusion of French ingredients and techniques. Pho (soup), bun (vermicelli noodles), and banh mi sandwiches have every component one could desire: crunchy, spicy, sweet, salty, and of course the rich umami flavor that makes the dishes "close-your-eyes" good. Restaurant BT is a can't-miss spot, possibly the only French-Vietnamese restaurant in the area and, fortunately for us diners, it's an outstanding example of the cuisine.

Byblos Cafe, 2832 S. MacDill Ave., Tampa, FL 33629; (813) 805-7977; bybloscafe.com; Lebanese/Middle Eastern; $$$. Sultry music, dim lights, vividly colored walls, exotic women dancing around tables. . . . No, I'm not describing a gentleman's club. This (actually quite classy) establishment is called Byblos, and it offers up some of the best Lebanese food in the area. The dancers are belly dancers who entertain guests while they nosh on specialties such as *soujouk* (spicy sausage), *kibbeh nayeh* (raw beef with cracked bulgar), and tabbouleh (parsley salad). Byblos also has top-notch outdoor seating, with comfortable chairs under a covered awning and fans to keep customers cool in the hot months. Recommended for great al fresco dining, ideally lunch in the cooler months or dinner in the warmer.

Cappy's Pizzeria, 3200 W. Bay to Bay Blvd., Tampa, FL 33629; (813) 835-0785; cappyspizzaonline.com; Pizza; $$. If you're in search of a really excellent deep-dish pizza, Cappy's is the place to go. Sister restaurant to Pinky's, Cappy's is a very laid-back, lost-in-time, almost hipster-y spot that has a very simple menu: New York–style pizza, Chicago-style pizza, salad, and calzones. The NY-style pie is tasty, but with Paci's and Pane Rustica making such stellar thin-crust pie in the immediate vicinity, Chicago deep dish is the way to go. Rumor has it only a very few select people know the recipe to the dough/crust, and they come and make it each day for all four of Cappy's locations. The pie is excellent, the tomato sauce is perfectly salted/seasoned, the cheese is just thick enough that it offers a bit of a gooey dimension without turning the pie into a rubbery mess like one might find in a lot of national chains. Cappy's is my favorite Chicago-style pizza in Tampa and has been for years. It's well worth a shot if a big, thick steak of a pizza is what you're in the mood for.

Ceviche, 2500 W. Azeele St., Tampa, FL 33606; (813) 250-0203; ceviche.com; Tapas; $$$. One of the most fun restaurants to eat at in the area is Ceviche. One of South Tampa's first tapas bars, Ceviche outgrew its first space fairly quickly (which is now occupied by a really fun speakeasy called **Ciro's** [below]) and has changed locations twice from the growth associated with the popularity of the concept. Live music on weekends, a hip atmosphere, and a dance floor make this restaurant an enticing destination for any occasion, day or night. There is a separate dining area should you not be interested in the music, and it also doubles as a great space to use for a party. The menu is impressively extensive and has over a hundred items at a wide variety of portion sizes and price points, focusing on classic Spanish fare. Al fresco dining is also available, and tables have retractable umbrellas should you (or should you not) want to soak up some beautiful Florida sunshine. Ceviche is also a great place to start out a fun night with friends, given that its newest location is a very short walk from the Howard Avenue bar scene.

Ciro's Speakeasy and Supper Club, 2109 Bayshore Blvd., Tampa, FL 33606; (813) 251-0022; Modern American/French; $$$. I really shouldn't discuss this next restaurant, unless you know the password. Only kidding! Ciro's is Tampa's worst-kept secret, a speakeasy that makes classic pre-Prohibition cocktails and some darn yummy food, too. It is located in a condominium building at the very south end of Howard Avenue, and oddly enough for a speakeasy, valet parking is available. Upon approaching the unmarked door and knocking, a young man or woman will greet you and request a password, which unfortunately isn't "Swordfish." Or "Fidelio." Truthfully, you may not be able to get in without calling first to make a reservation and obtaining a password from whomever you speak to on the phone, but I assure you, all the trouble is worth it. Upon walking in, you'll notice the interior is quite dark (it'll take your eyes a moment to adjust), so the owners cleverly made menus that light up when opened, which is a cool effect, even before having a few cocktails. Dining takes place primarily in private booths, while the bar area is geared more toward fans of fine libations. The mixologists at Ciro's are very well trained in making some very classic cocktails (please, don't go in and order a "rum and coke," this isn't that type of establishment), and the food menu has everything from the elegant to the outlandish, such as filet tartare, duck fat french fries, truffled popcorn, even pork belly pizza! An evening at Ciro's will be one not soon forgotten and is highly recommended.

Datz, 2616 S. MacDill Ave., Tampa, FL 33629; (813) 831-7000; datz deli.com; Gastropub/Comfort Food; $$. **Datz** could very well be the most interesting restaurant in South Tampa, after being open only a few short years. Owners Suzanne and Roger Perry have iterated the concept multiple times in an effort to grow with feedback from their loyal customers. Although not every transition was smooth, the growth certainly paid off considering the restaurant consistently pops up as a favorite in local blogs, newspapers, and magazines, and has been in the top five restaurants on Urbanspoon for years. Love the microbrews? Try one of 40 rotating drafts. Big fan of wine?

 Nearly every wall (and the chandeliers) are loaded with racks of bottles, and there's a cellar for rare goodies, too. Cocktails your thing? Datz carries only artisan spirits, liqueurs, and ingredients, and even flew in a well-known mixologist from NYC to train the bar staff. Now wait, there's something missing here . . . oh yes, the food! Datz may be best known for creative and generously portioned sandwiches (you may want to split one with a friend) such as their take on the Cuban sandwich, the "Havana Hottie": smoked pulled pork, house-baked ham, spicy honeycup mustard, and jarlsberg cheese, piled plentifully on a batard and pressed until crispy and melty. Although Datz started as a deli in its infancy, it has become more of a gastropub in its adulthood. Check out the menu for items like mac n' cheese stuffed meat loaf, fried chicken and waffles, and "the piggy" flatbread, which are quickly becoming frequently requested staples. Breakfast and

brunch are equally impressive; if you're bored with traditional pan-cakes, Datz offers them in the red velvet variety, drizzled with cream cheese icing and accompanied by Neuske's thick-cut applewood smoked bacon. The fun doesn't stop there—the restaurant hosts many food-related and beer/wine/spirit events and has something fun to do nearly every week. See Chef Heather Stalker's recipes for **Datz Eberson's Old Fashioned, Datz Bacon Mac N' Cheese, Barry C's Mac N' Cheese Stuffed Meat Loaf Poutine,** and **Pastrami Pork Belly** starting on p. 225.

Doormet, 1155 S. Dale Mabry Hwy., Tampa, FL 33629; (813) 287-3667; doormet.com; American/Sandwiches/Salads; $$. Doormet is an odd name, no? Let's shed some light on that. South Tampa natives and restaurant veterans, the Koch brothers wanted to create a restaurant that could bring gourmet fare to your door, and thus Doormet (pronounced door-may) was born. Although Doormet's specialty is delivery (they can even deliver beer and wine!), they have around a dozen tables for dine-in service and offer up some very fresh and very tasty American fare that they've elevated quite a bit. Pizzas such as the "Quattro" have chèvre, fontina, Parmesan, and cheddar cheeses accompanied by basil pesto and a balsamic reduction, while sandwiches like the "Tomozza" have a fantastic mix of ingredients such as baby mozzarella, prosciutto, tomato, and pesto (also with that delectable balsamic drizzle!). While the salads, sandwiches, pizzas, and soups are dependably excellent at Doormet, the weekly specials are frequently a big hit in the foodie commu-nity and have garnered the Koch brothers quite a following. Recent creations such as their truffled mac n' cheese make local media "Can't Miss" lists frequently and justly so; it's amazing. An added bonus, the owners are big wine and craft beer aficionados, which makes for an impressive selection of both microbrews and elegant wines, all at very reasonable prices. If you love good food but just don't feel like leaving the house, or can't make lunch because everything is crazy at the office, Doormet will bring something fresh and delicious right over.

Edison Food & Drink Lab, 912 W. Kennedy Blvd., Tampa, FL 33606; (813) 254-7111; edison-tampa.com; Modern American; $$$$. Jeannie Pierola is back. Jeannie is one of Tampa's rock-star chefs who has garnered more local media buzz than nearly any other chef in the Bay in years. Former executive chef of both **Sidebern's** (p. 28) and **Bern's Steakhouse** (p. 34), Jeannie parted ways with the restaurants in 2007 and remained quiet, with much buzz about where she would go or what she would do. Fast forward to 2010, and Jeannie pioneered the pop-up dinner concept in Tampa, using various restaurants' kitchens in South Tampa to serve dinners for a few weeks at a time and then once again going silent until the next iteration of her concept, which was very creative dishes utilizing molecular gastronomy and less common ingredients. Fast forward to 2012: Pierola opens a stationary restaurant in the space formerly occupied by Knife & Company with a similar menu theme to her pop-up dinners with very artful dishes bordering on experimental. The space has a contemporary but inviting feel that can be dressed up or dressed down given the occasion, and little nuance decorations add to the "Lab" portion of the name, such as beakers used for flower vases and wine carafes. One of the most impressive aspects of the restaurant is the extremely small kitchen in which she concocts some of the most cutting-edge food in all of Tampa Bay. The menu changes frequently, but be sure to try the vanilla-scented *foie gras* on shrimp toasts, and the duck confit and *foie gras* tacos, should you get the opportunity.

Floridian Cuban Sandwiches, 4424 W. Kennedy Blvd., Tampa, FL 33609; (813) 287-6662; finestcubansandwich.com; Sandwiches; $. The Floridian specializes in Cuban sandwiches. This fact is very important given that there are literally hundreds of places in Tampa to get a Cuban sandwich, and very few focus the majority of their energy on the sandwich itself. So often restaurants herald their Cuban sandwich as a draw or marketing ploy (I guarantee you'll see at least a dozen that claim theirs to be "Best in the Bay") and follow suit with an expansive menu that tends to pull focus and love away from their shining star, that pressed beauty of a sandwich that Tampa does better than any other city in the world. All that said, the Floridian is a quirkily decorated little sandwich shop with half a dozen tables and adorned with murals of enormous leaves surrounded by pastel shades of blue. Goofy decoration aside, Floridian gets high marks for keeping the focus of the restaurant and of their menu on the Cuban, with a handful of other items that

Cuban Sandwiches

Who could write about Tampa without showing love to one of the most amazing sandwiches on the planet? The Cuban sandwich debuted in the USA right here in Tampa, in Ybor City. A Cuban sandwich starts with the bread. Real Cuban bread is baked at dozens of bakeries in Tampa, but locals consider **La Segunda Central**'s bread to be the best. The bread is split open, yellow mustard is spread inside, and sliced pickles are distributed evenly prior to laying down a layer of swiss cheese. Meat includes sliced ham, roast pork, and Genoa salami. Versions of the sandwich found outside of Tampa typically don't include the salami; it's believed that ingredient came from the influence of Italian immigrants in Tampa. Close the bread, brush the outside with a bit of butter, and press it (the press is called a "plancha") until the bread toasts slightly, the juices distribute, and the cheese layer melts. Voila, you are holding a toasty, delicious bit of history! If anyone ever makes you a Cuban with lettuce and tomato on it, or a slathering blob of mayo, immediately throw it back at them—you've bought a fake! It might also be good to run after throwing it at them, in case they're upset and/or bigger than you. The sandwich was a popular lunch for Cuban immigrants working at cigar factories in Ybor City, while just the buttered Cuban bread made for a yummy breakfast coupled with a *cafe con leche* (equal parts espresso/bold coffee and scalded milk). A trip to Tampa without trying a Cuban sandwich would be an incomplete trip!

complement it (such as their excellent Floridian mixed-bean soup with bacon, or their rich, herby, and viscous black bean soup). La Segunda bread is used (which any Cuban sandwich purist will tell you is the best of the best), a quick brush of butter, and a good 5-minute press makes the sandwich come out perfect: crunchy bread with soft insides, each meat high enough quality that it would be tasty on its own, but when combined with pickles and mustard and a few slices of gooey swiss cheese (thanks to the generous press) it's heaven on a loaf.

Hula Bay Club, 5210 W. Tyson Ave., Tampa, FL 33611; (813) 837-4852; hulabayclub.com; Seafood/Sushi; $$$. Occupying the space formerly known as Rattlefish, Hula Bay Club is an even trendier, even more fun iteration of its predecessor. Focusing on very approachable menu items such as burgers, sushi, seafood, and a raw bar, HBC is the place to go with friends for a meal and drinks before a night out on the town. The interior is Hawaiian themed (naturally) with palms and bamboo accents, and the deck is a fantastic place to sit and watch boats slip around while the sun sets. If you've been out on a boat for the day working up an appetite, you can pull right up and dock at the restaurant, or at the neighboring marina. Live music, waterfront dining, and yummy grub make Hula Bay Club a great choice for someone looking for dinner with a view.

Kojak's House of Ribs, 2808 W. Gandy Blvd., Tampa, FL 33611; (813) 837-3774; kojaksbbq.net; Barbecue; $$. Ribs. Don't come to Kojak's for anything else. This isn't a health food store, this isn't a place to enjoy cocktails with your friends and discuss life, this is a House of Ribs. A very no-frills restaurant, Kojak's plays up its strengths and pays little heed to its weaknesses, its strength being ribs and desserts. Smokey, tender, well spiced, and super flavorful, the ribs at this little 30-plus-year-old South Tampa staple are among the best in the area. Open for lunch and dinner every day except Mon, Kojak's is a great place to pop in and have a rib platter with a sweet iced tea, and maybe a slice of chocolate lava cake if you deserve a treat.

Love's Artifacts Bar and Grille, 4914 S. MacDill Ave., Tampa, FL 33611; (813) 831-3273; loves.sparxoo.com; American; $$. How many restaurants do you know that were previously a car dealership? Of those, how many never changed ownership when transitioning from a car dealership to a restaurant? My guess would be "none," but maybe I'm wrong. Lynn Love fell victim to the economy as did many other car dealers and used his love for food to convert "Love's Used Cars" into "Love's Artifacts Bar and Grille," a very eclectic eatery. Upon entering the interior, one might think that the owners robbed a number of elderly people from the show *Hoarders* and took anything they could and glued it to the walls. Southern favorites pepper the menu, along with Love's own specialties such as the brie quesadilla, the "Fat Italian" sandwich, or the very curious peanut butter–stuffed jalapeños. Yes, those are all real menu items, and they're all quite tasty. Brunch at Love's is one of the best bargains in Tampa, only $9.95 for all-you-can-eat fried chicken, collards, mac n' cheese, bacon, etc., and for another $6.95 you get unlimited booze, too. That may be the best brunch buffet deal in South Tampa.

Mad Dogs & Englishmen, 4115 S. MacDill Ave., Tampa, FL 33611; (813) 832-3037; maddogs.com; British/Gastropub; $$$. Mad Dogs & Englishmen is a unique creature. The restaurant is somewhere between a British pub and a gastropub (don't let the words "British food" scare you; it's actually quite good) and has fantastic outdoor seating under a trellis-esque canopy from which white lights are strewn. Menu favorites include the lobster salad and the steak sandwich, both of which go down quite well with a draft beer. The owner can often be found on one side of the bar or the other and is a real nice guy, very entertaining to speak to. The sweet potato fries are on par with narcotics when it comes to addictiveness, by the way; whatever you may order, getting a side of those would be highly advised.

Osteria Natalina, 3215 S. MacDill Ave., Tampa, FL 33629; (813) 831-1210; osterianatalina.com; Italian; $$$. Osteria Natalina (formerly Spartaco) at first glance is an unassuming Italian restaurant tucked away in a strip mall near a highway overpass. The caveat? It's considered by most foodies to be the best Italian restaurant in South Tampa and, by some, best in the entire city. Although it's a small spot, big flavors are abundant, and if you have a favorite Italian dish not on the menu, the chefs are typically willing to make it for you, assuming they have the ingredients. The bread kicks off the meal with a bang, accompanied by a unique garlic and olive tapenade that will make you wish all Italian restaurants put that much love into something as simple as the bread course. Pasta is al dente and sauces are worth swooning over. Proteins are top quality and perfectly cooked. This is Italian food as it should be, true to style and crafted by an Italian chef! Osteria is a must for any lover of Italian fare.

Paci's Pizza, 2307 S. Dale Mabry Hwy., Tampa, FL 33629; (813) 253-2973; pacispizza.com; Pizza; $$. Paci's Pizza is unquestionably one of the very best (if not THE very best) New York–style pizza spots in Tampa. Dough and sauce are both made in house using bottled water, and toppings are fresh and simple. Owner Skip Glass crafts nearly every pie you'll have the pleasure of eating and is a friendly guy with a good disposition, which is fortunate considering he's built like a professional wrestler! I sure wouldn't want him mad at me, but given that he makes so many people happy with his amazing pies, I can understand why he seems to always be in a good mood. As a favor to the author, please, don't even think of getting your pizza to go. Paci's doesn't deliver because pizza this thin doesn't travel well. You tend to lose the crunch, the aromatics of the pie right out of the oven; a lot of the subtle nuances that make pizza so amazing exist only in a ten-minute window, so enjoy it as soon as it's cool enough to eat. A truly fantastic pizza needs nearly nothing on top of it as the quality of the primary ingredients shine brightest in their pure form. Paci's Margherita is a perfect example of this with only tomato sauce, baby mozzarella, fresh basil, and olive oil on top of lightly blackened crust. Exquisite. Bring a friend though; the pizza comes in only one size, and it isn't small (it barely fits on the table). If you're extra hungry or really need some protein, Skip makes a pie with slices of huge meatballs and dollops of ricotta cheese that is also admittedly fantastic, and the cannolis are shipped in fresh directly from the Big Apple—they're probably the best in town.

Pane Rustica, 3225 S. MacDill Ave., Tampa, FL 33629; (813) 902-8828; panerusticabakery.com; Modern American; $$$. If you haven't eaten at Pane Rustica before, kindly stop what you are doing and GO. This bakery/cafe in an unassuming strip mall on South MacDill Avenue has many items local foodies consider to be the best in the Bay. Thin-crust wood-fired pizzas, each masterfully created by the pizza artist, may feature toppings such as duck, goat cheese, roasted garlic, radicchio, spinach, basil, sun-dried tomatoes, etc. You get the idea: Whatever seems freshest and most delicious at the time goes on the pie, into the oven, and voila, magic is born. As amazing as it is, the pizza is merely the tip of the iceberg. The best way to order lunch at Pane is to get the single white page of daily specials (printed daily, naturally), which changes every day and is never the same two days in a row, and pick whatever your heart desires. Lunch is an absolute bargain; most items are $14 or less, with dishes like tricolored butternut squash lobster ravioli, filet tips in gnocchi and a marsala cream, or for braver souls, the "Shut Up and Eat" entree, which is completely at the chef's discretion. (An author's note: Please don't ask what's in the Shut Up and Eat. Employees get asked that question dozens of times each day, and they don't have a clue.) Save room for dessert: Pane Rustica's baked goods are amazing. Many tout their cupcakes to

be the best in Tampa, and just about any of their sweet delicacies is sure to please. While lunch is very casual and relaxed, dinner at Pane takes on a more elegant atmosphere, and the dishes (and prices) follow suit. Candlelit tables, attentive service, and a wonderful selection of wines and spirits make this restaurant perfect for an intimate occasion and are sure to impress. If lunch is the plan, showing up early would be highly recommended as it can get a bit crowded closer to noon, and if attending for dinner (especially on weekends), reservations are a must.

Pinky's Diner, 3203 W. Bay to Bay Blvd., Tampa, FL 33629; (813) 831-9339; pinkysdiner.com; Breakfast/Lunch; $. Pinky's makes a pancake sandwich. That really ought to be all you need to read, but should that not be convincing enough, let me tell you a bit about the spot where the locals eat breakfast. Across the street from equally eclectic and tasty **Cappy's Pizzeria** (p. 86), Pinky's Diner is a breakfast/lunch-only spot that makes classic breakfast and lunch items (pancakes, griddled goodies, etc., for breakfast, and salads and sandwiches for lunch), with a bit of panache to separate them from your typical "greasy spoon." Diners line up early on weekends, many to eat away their hangovers, and often are seen waiting outside because Pinky's doesn't take reservations. Bear that in mind when making your plans, as it is a very small space.

Queen of Sheba Ethiopian Restaurant, 3636 Henderson Blvd., Tampa, FL 33609; (813) 872-6000; ethiopianrestauranttampa.com; Ethiopian; $$. Queen of Sheba offers some of the most authentic, non-Westernized cuisine in all of South Tampa. Ethiopian cuisine to be more precise. True-to-style food is presented in a fun and comfortable setting; Queen of Sheba is not only delicious but can also be an adventure for the diners! The restaurant is staffed by friendly servers who are very accommodating and patient with first-timers. You may even have the owner herself come out and explain the cuisine and traditions to you, and offer you a very refreshing Ethiopian beer to complement your food. The lack of silverware on the table isn't an error; food is typically handled, assembled, and eaten using *injera* (a thin purple sourdough crepe-like pancake). Tear off a palm-sized piece of *injera* and grab a handful of vegetables or meat, but be prepared for the explosion of flavor that will soon follow! The fare at Queen of Sheba is anything but bland, with spices, herbs, and heat prevalent in the dishes, which range from vegetarian-friendly to a carnivore's dream. If it's your first visit, the sampler platter is an excellent choice and makes for a memorable meal that will impress friends or even your new date!

Schiller's German Deli, 4327 W. El Prado Blvd., Tampa, FL 33629; (813) 839-6666; German; $. Schiller's German Deli is a South Tampa staple, a family business over six decades old and one that never strayed far from the original concept. A small handful of restaurants in South Tampa are more than half a century old, and most deserve to be so. Schiller's offers a plethora of imported German beers, meats, chocolates, candies, and best of all, authentic sandwiches. Coupled with their homemade breads and toppings straight from Deutschland, the quality meats, sausages, krauts, and other goodies make Schiller's lunch a fantastic treat, presented in a very simple European deli atmosphere. If you're a fan of European beers, you've come to the right place. Schiller's has a vast array of different European beers (the majority of which are German, naturally); have the very knowledgeable staff help you select one to wash down their truly excellent Reuben sandwich. Probably the "wurst" thing you could do would be to miss out on the homemade apple strudel!

Sidebern's, 2208 W. Morrison Ave., Tampa, FL 33606; (813) 258-2233; sideberns.com; Modern American; $$$$. Sidebern's may be the best restaurant in Tampa. The name has nothing to do with facial hair—it is a sister restaurant to the world-famous Bern's Steakhouse and is very contemporary while its older brother remains quite classic. The decor is downright sexy—sleek, colorful yet sultry, very modern, with a wiry chandelier hanging over the triangular-shaped bar that is a thing of beauty. Shapes are a prominent theme throughout the restaurant; even the wooden bar has different-colored orbs of wood embedded into it. Sidebern's employs some of the most talented food-people in all of Tampa Bay, from their in-house cheese expert to their national award–winning mixologist bar manager, to the James Beard–nominated chef. Even the attached wine shop is managed by a sommelier who is a very likable guy with a keen palate. The menu changes quite frequently and is very cutting edge in its use of ingredients. Everything appears from rabbits to duck hearts (worry not, less-adventurous eaters have numerous options and the steak at SB is to die for), and the cheese selection is rivaled by few restaurants anywhere. If one has a "penchant for fromage," this would be the perfect place to indulge and explore. Another very respectable and enticing quality about the food is that as many of the ingredients as possible are sourced locally, and the farms and dairies that are used are printed on the menu. The restaurant has great weekly events at the wine shop, such as the "Crush Hour" where for $25 one can try a multitude of high-end wines and pair them with some very nice cheese, and "Potluck Wednesday," where a delicious to-go dinner is available for only $20 and a few wines are featured for free tasting. Want an insider tip on how to enjoy this amazing restaurant and not spend a ton? Happy hour! Sidebern's happy hour is a very well-known secret among foodies in

EAT LOCAL

The Eat Local scene has been picking up momentum in Tampa Bay and is a great movement to get behind. Eating local often costs no more than not doing so, but it supports local farmers that are putting a lot more love into growing and raising food for people that is also tastier and healthier for them. Florida has a great climate for growing a wide variety of different foodstuffs, and the growing season is longer here than in many other parts of the USA given the warm climate, with some foods available nearly year-round. Some great restaurants in Tampa that support the Eat Local movement are The Refinery, Sideberns, Pelagia Trattoria, Boca, and Cafe Dufrain. There are numerous others; these are just a few the author is quite fond of and that have made a significant contribution to the Tampa food scene by sourcing as much of (in many cases nearly all of) their food from farms in the area. Tampa also has local coffee roasters (Buddy Brew, Kahwa), local breweries (Cigar City, Dunedin Brewery, Seventh Sun), and more. Supporting local keeps small-business owners in business, creates new jobs, and improves the community in general!

the Bay. Every day except Sunday (they're closed Sun) from 5 to 7 p.m. there is a bar menu with 6 fantastic small plates, 6 creative cocktails, 6 different wines, and 6 craft beers, all at $5 each! Couple that with the very friendly and professional bartending staff and you've got the best HH Tampa has to offer. Highly highly highly recommended. See Chef Chad Johnson's recipes for **Roasted Gulf, BBQ Ceviche, Roasted Asparagus,** and **Beef Cheek Ravioli** starting on p. 231.

Square 1 Burgers, 3701 Henderson Blvd., Tampa, FL 33607; (813) 414-0101; square1burgers.com; Burgers; $$. Square 1 was one of the first burger spots in South Tampa to tackle the newer "gourmet burger" trend, and they did so quite well. All grass-fed, hormone-free beef comprises even the most basic of burgers, with options to elevate your selection to the elite Kobe beef, or even go outside the box and try their buffalo, lamb, chicken, or tuna burgers. Fries are available in standard form and also in the extra-delicious sweet-potato variety, with numerous unique dipping sauces that can make for pretty entertaining flavor experiments. Not a meat-eater? Square 1 didn't forget about you; they have a number of vegetarian choices from por-tobello burgers to gruyère grilled cheese sandwiches. If all that wasn't enticing enough, there's a full bar and plenty of beer and wine choices should you need an adult beverage to wash down that tasty burger.

TC Choy, 301 S. Howard Ave., Tampa, FL 33606; (813) 251-1191; tcchoysbistro.com; Asian/Dim Sum; $$. Cantonese cuisine is a dynamic, comforting mélange of flavors ranging from spicy to salty to sweet to funky. Arguably the best and most authentic Cantonese/

Chinese food in South Tampa is TC Choy's Asian bistro, and it's also one of the better decorated. The interior is beautiful with fish tanks artfully embedded into glass tile walls, huge dragon murals, and a large open stainless-steel kitchen that adds a very clean, modern dimension to the room. The dim sum lunch is truly impressive, especially on weekends. Young servers push around various stainless-steel carts with no identifier as to what lies within, so as the server comes by your table he or she will lift the top off a number of small steam trays filled with everything from simple and tasty *shumai* (dumplings) to more adventurous foods such as chicken feet or tripe. There are multiple steam carts, a soup cart, a fried goodies cart, and the "kitchen special" cart which has entree-size dishes, if a larger dish is what you're looking for. A recommendation: bring some friends and try as much as you can! Things that may sound strange might end up being delicious, so take an opportunity to eat outside your comfort zone and give this excellent Asian bistro a go.

Thai Market and Kitchen, 3325 S. Dale Mabry Hwy., Tampa, FL 33629; (813) 837-5735; thaimarketkitchen.com; Thai; $. While Thai Market and Kitchen may not be winning any awards for aesthetics, they have certainly caught the attention of local foodies who seek out authentic, spicy, and affordable Thai food. Only a few tables are available for dining in, and at lunchtime they are often filled with content Asian customers who are focused on their food and conversations. When seeking out authentic ethnic food, I usually feel successful when I stumble into an eatery where I'm the only person not of that ethnicity. At Thai Market, I feel pretty successful; when

English isn't the first language, there's a much higher probability what you're about to eat hasn't been dumbed-down for the Western palate. Soups, noodle dishes, curry, dumplings—most anything you order will be tasty, and after your meal feel free to explore the market for sauces, seasonings, and other hard-to-find ingredients to give Thai cooking at home a try.

Wimauma, 4205 S. MacDill Ave., Tampa, FL 33611; (813) 793-1687; wimaumafoods.com; Modern Southern; $$$. A mom-and-pop restaurant with hyper-talented Chef Gary Moran (who knifed at famous restaurants such as Le Bernadin and Bouley in New York City), a gentleman as eccentric as he is skilled. Wimauma shares the name of another nearby small town in Florida, so when looking for it using Google Maps, be sure to type "Restaurant Wimauma." The menu is Southern meets fine dining, yet in a very casual atmosphere. The couple is a big proponent of the Eat Local movement and sources as much local meat and dairy as possible, while growing much of their herbs and veggies in the land behind the restaurant. Expect menu items such as fried oysters with house-smoked tomato jam on guacamole, smoked duck spring rolls with green papaya slaw and sweet lime chili dipping sauce, or decadent desserts like a chocolate bacon brownie with butter pecan ice cream and basil chantilly. Yes, you read all that right. At the time of writing this, Wimauma has been open only for a handful of months but has already skyrocketed to the top of the restaurant-buzz list and continues to impress diners with its ever-changing and inimitable menu items. See Chef Moran's recipes for **Black Pepper Gravy, Collard Greens, Crispy Fried Florida Oysters, Jalapeño-Cheddar Spoonbread**, and **Pickled Peaches** starting on p. 219.

Landmarks

Bern's, 1208 S. Howard Ave., Tampa, FL 33606; (813) 251-2421; bernssteakhouse.com; Steak House; $$$$. Bern Laxer christened Bern's Steakhouse over 50 years ago in South Tampa and has since been called one of the best steak houses in the USA on dozens of occasions, sometimes even #1. Many US presidents have dined at the restaurant, as have celebrities, comedians, and professional athletes. Today Bern's son David runs the restaurant, which has dozens if not hundreds of servers, multiple sommeliers, an enormous kitchen staff, and a number of managers to keep everything organized. The wine list is worthy of note, as Bern's has the largest wine selection of any restaurant on planet Earth. No joke. Their offsite cellar holds over half a million bottles of wine, ranging in age from a year old to over two hundred years old, and in price from $20 to $20,000. The wine selection isn't the only impressive selection though, as the menu has over a dozen caviars to choose from, numerous soups, salads, and vegetables, and a "Kitchen Within a Kitchen" menu of daily seasonal and fresh creations. I suppose this brings us to the steak, right? Filet mignon, chateaubriand, strip sirloin, delmonico, porterhouse, and T-bone are your choices, in a variety of thicknesses, all broiled over charcoal to the doneness you specify.

A personal favorite is the special chateaubriand cooked "Pittsburgh" medium-rare and shared with a bottle of wine and some great conversation.

The Colonnade, 3401 Bayshore Blvd., Tampa, FL 33629; (813) 839-7558, thenade.com; Seafood; $$$. The Colonnade is a South Tampa landmark that is over 75 years old! Initially a burgers n' fries joint, the 'Nade switched to serving seafood after the founder's son, Jack Whiteside, returned from being stationed in San Francisco (and falling in love with West Coast seafood) during World War II. Today a popular spot for a quiet meal, and also one of the very few restaurants on Bayshore Boulevard looking out into the Bay, The Colonnade is a great place to soak up a bit of South Tampa history. With a pretty sizable seafood-centric menu, diners have a great number of choices, but make sure to save room for their well-known Key lime pie, homemade each day.

Mise en Place, 442 W. Kennedy Blvd., Tampa, FL 33606; (813) 254-5373; miseonline.com; French/Modern American; $$$$. Meaning "everything in its place," Mise en Place is a culinary term that refers to a chef having his or her ingredients portioned out and prepared so that in a time-sensitive recipe they won't have to lose precious minutes to additional preparation. Although probably just a clever name, the Tampa restaurant Mise en Place has been making very trendy and contemporary food for over 25 years now. The interior is beautiful, modern architecture, glass tiles with gold accents, a sexy bar, and multiple sections of seating that really helps separate private parties and events. Menu items are over the top with highlights such as aleppo spice-rubbed duck with wild mushroom *foie gras* cannelloni or sous vide venison loin with andouille rabbit *maque choux* and smoked tomato jus. Don't worry if you can't pronounce everything; just make sure you try it!

Wright's Gourmet House, 1200 S. Dale Mabry Hwy., Tampa, FL 33629; (813) 253-3838; wrightsgourmet.com; Sandwiches; $. Wright's Gourmet House is another South Tampa institution, nearing half a century old. The interior is very much a deli, and ordering takes place in front of big glass cases that house yummy-looking salads and sides. While hungry diners come in and eye the chalkboards overhead for the selection that will soon become their meal, behind the counter employees busily assemble and press some very unique sandwiches dreamed up by the Wright family decades before. House specialties like the "Beef Martini" sandwich (rare roast beef, mushrooms, bacon, and herbed garlic spread) or classics like the Cuban sandwich (which has legitimately won multiple awards as one of the best in Tampa and is also one of my favorites) are consistently great and safe bets for a great lunch. No alcohol is served, but a number of different classic sodas and iced teas are available. Wright's bakes some fantastic cakes and other sweet treats, in all sizes from "snack" to "party," which tend to make you pretty popular wherever you may take them. As with many good lunch spots that are in proximity to both the Westshore Business District and MacDill Air Force Base, Wright's gets pretty busy during lunch so showing up half an hour early is never a bad decision!

Specialty Stores, Markets & Producers

Buddy Brew Coffee, 2020 W. Kennedy Blvd., Tampa, FL 33606; (813) 258-2739; buddybrew.com. Buddy Brew Coffee is a very unassuming coffee shop that has accomplished an awful lot in the short time they've been open. Small-batch coffee, artisan roasted in-house and expertly served, BBC has converted more than a few people from being fans of the national chains over to truly appreciating the subtle nuance and flavor of what coffee should actually taste like. The baristas at the BBC shop are some of the most impressive in the Bay, making drinks very patiently and with great precision, but thankfully without pretentiousness. The difference between what you'll get at Buddy Brew versus what you get at a national chain is that you have an artisan roaster roast your beans to the perfect temperature for the perfect period of time, right there in the store. It's said that a roasted bean stays at peak flavor up to two weeks, but the national chains typically have beans that were roasted three or more weeks prior, and in huge batches, so if that mass-produced java in your cup tastes burnt, it probably is. Maybe it's time to see what your brew can do for you?

Castellano & Pizzo, 4200 Henderson Blvd., Tampa, FL 33629; (813) 289-5275; castellanoandpizzo.com. Castellano & Pizzo started life in the 1890s in Ybor City and existed there until the 1970s, when it changed its location to South Tampa. A gourmet market for Italian and Spanish delicacies, C&P's deli counter alone should make you hungry shortly after you walk through the front door. Imported oils, coffees, pastas, bottled waters, olives, canned meats, and more are available, along with a great cheese and wine selection (Italian focused, of course). Mon through Fri the cafe is open for lunch and whips up some delicious Italian classics as well as some specialties of the week, and there are weekly wine tastings.

Cheese Please, 4213 S. Manhattan Ave., Tampa, FL 33611; (813) 805-2743; cheesepleasetampa.com. One of Tampa's few artisan cheese stores, Cheese Please has something for everyone. If you want mild or stinky, soft or hard, domestic or international, it's available there, along with a number of jams, jellies, honeys, and other fun complements. Cheese Please holds tastings and wine pairings on Fri, which are delicious fun and well worth a visit if you're in the area!

Farm in the City, 6032 S. 2nd St., Tampa, FL 33611. Many people have lived nearly their whole lives in South Tampa and have no idea that there is a large farm only minutes away from them where they can buy local honey, free range eggs, and raw milk. The Farm in the City is a fun place to visit too, maybe even an educational one. Pigs, cows, horses, chickens, bees, and possums are just a few of the animals that can be found there, along with the slightly off-kilter owner/operator Marion, who is either fearless or a bit crazy, but a very nice and accommodating tour guide nonetheless. The honey is one of the first things visible upon approaching the farm, as it is in a stand at the street. Bottles are around $5 on the honor system. After heading in past the gate, one comes upon a glass-door refrigerator filled with free range eggs and raw milk, $5 and $10 respectively, again on the honor system. Veggies are also available and on occasion chickens and pigs, but the author would recommend you work that out with Marion in advance.

Oxford Exchange, 420 W. Kennedy Blvd., Tampa, FL 33606; (813) 253-0222; oxfordexchange.com. Millions of dollars went into building one of the most modern and beautiful spaces to relax and get coffee or tea, or enjoy a locally sourced, organic breakfast or lunch. Oxford Exchange opened in late 2012 and is more than a coffee or tea bar; it is also a restaurant, an event space (with a retractable glass ceiling in its beautiful indoor garden seating area!), and a bookstore. The space seems almost like something from New York City, no expense was spared on any component of the build, and the designers really nailed the look and feel they were going for. A tea bar serving TeBella tea sits across a coffee bar serving Buddy Brew coffee, both of which are operated by the respective owners of **TeBella** (p. 64) and **Buddy Brew** (p. 37). The dining space is as clean and modern as its menu, reasonably priced and focusing on locally sourced and organic ingredients. Afternoon tea is available from 2:30 to 5 p.m., and feel free to bring a bottle of wine to enjoy in the beautiful indoor garden; there is no corkage fee! As polished as a space can possibly be, Oxford Exchange manages to remain very inviting and alluring without being stuffy, and it is walking distance from Downtown Tampa and the University of Tampa to boot.

Ravioli Company, 3413 S. Manhattan Ave., Tampa, FL 33629; (813) 254-2051; raviolicompany.biz. Ravioli Company is South Tampa's source for handmade artisan pasta and ravioli. Whatever your pleasure, be it tortelloni, gnocchi, rigatoni, cavatelli, or even just high-quality spaghetti, Ravioli Company whips up some of the best pastas in the bay. Ravioli is, of course, their specialty though, with varieties such as sweet potato, butternut squash, goat cheese and fig, and even roast duck and truffled berry! If you're looking to impress friends at a party, or just to cook a heck of a meal at home, this is the place to pick up your pasta.

Robert's Meats, 3435 S. Westshore Blvd., Tampa, FL 33629; (813) 832-3584. Robert's Meats is one of the few dedicated butchers in South Tampa, and they're definitely worth visiting. If you need burgers ground from filet trimmings, steaks, high-quality sausages, a plethora of meats, or just the spices and condiments necessary for your barbecue, Robert's can help you out. Another great lesser-known fact about Robert's is that they will also prepare a lot of the food for you right there at the shop, and they make some great steak sandwiches. The biscuits and gravy is the true hidden treasure there, guaranteed to induce a food coma by the time you get home, so don't plan anything for the rest of the afternoon!

Downtown Tampa, Ybor City, Harbour Island & Davis Island

Downtown Tampa, Ybor City, Harbour Island, and Davis Island are all very close to one another, yet all are extremely different in both look and feel. Downtown Tampa is a bustling area for business during the day, and although it can be rather quiet at night, the current and previous mayors helped beautify the area and make it much more enjoyable aesthetically. Millions were invested in parks and public spaces, and thanks to some impressive high-rise condo buildings, Downtown is now becoming a more active area *outside* of business hours. Ybor City has a rich history dating back to the late 1800s as a cigar manufacturing area, has been said to be the birthplace of the Cuban sandwich, and is home to one of Tampa's oldest restaurants, The Columbia. Davis Island is a primarily residential, small (approximately 1 square mile) island due south of Downtown Tampa, with a single bridge used to enter or leave. Many residents of Davis Island (or "D.I.," as it is often called) like to stay on the island and favor bicycles and golf carts as their means of transportation to get to local restaurants or markets when the weather allows. Harbour Island is similar to Davis Island but less than half the size and is primarily condos and hotels.

Foodie Faves

Acropolis Greek Taverna, 1833 E. 7th Ave., Tampa, FL 33605; (813) 242-4545; acropolistaverna.com; Greek; $$$. OPA! Nightly live music and (on weekends) belly dancers are two of the reasons that the Acropolis Greek Taverna is one of the most hoppin' spots in Ybor City. If you or someone you know is a fan of Greek food and wants a little entertainment with their meal, this would be the place to take them. The two-story interior is very inviting and open, large pieces of Greek art adorn the walls, and servers are very neatly dressed in all black. Menu items are mostly classic Greek dishes, seafood focused such as octopus and calamari, salted fish, grilled whole snapper, and more. Lamb and beef are both available, and the gyro plate with both is a great selection, as are the rest of their wraps. Try something fun and different like their drunken quail (chargrilled quail topped with lemon wine sauce and served with orzo and veggies). Greek food with live music and a free show? Sounds like a great start to a great weekend!

Bailey's Catering and Restaurant, 238 E. Davis Blvd., Tampa, FL 33606; (813) 254-8018; baileycatering.com; American; $$$. Kim Bailey has created something people love, crave, and need. His restaurant Bailey's serves up comfort food in a slightly elevated format, for both the more simple and advanced palates of locals and tourists alike. Now bear in mind that did say "comfort food," and unless you have a really hearty appetite, you may want to share some dishes here. Scratch that, just plan on sharing some dishes here; you'll want to save room for dessert, which is where Bailey really shines. That may be a task easier said than done, with menu items such as honey-drizzled buttermilk fried chicken with waffles (a Southern dish that is making a pretty awesome resurgence in Tampa Bay), or the "Mom's Best Ever Meat Loaf," which is a really healthy portion of some pretty straightforward, close-your-eyes-good meat loaf. Also not to miss are the powdered sugar–dusted corn fritters, and the classic sides (mashed potatoes, mac n' cheese, collards, green beans, etc.). The interior of the restaurant is halfway between a nice colonial home and a bistro, and the outdoor courtyard seating in front continues to exude the casual South, with a fountain and bistro-esque tables and chairs.

If you're a fan of Southern food but want a nice setting, Bailey's is a safe bet.

Bamboozle Cafe, 516 N. Tampa St., Tampa, FL 33602; (813) 223-7320; bamboozlecafe.com; Vietnamese; $$. Bamboozle Cafe did a fantastic service for Downtown diners by offering a very accessible format of Vietnamese cuisine, and it did so with a focus on fresh, healthy, seasonal ingredients. Thus far its concept has endured the test of time, and Downtown Tampa (where historically non-chain restaurants haven't fared well) has accepted it into its food bosom. When I say accessible, I don't mean dumbed-down per se, just that the food is presented in a way that may be more enticing to non-Asians who aren't familiar with the cuisine. The menu is filled with tasty selections, the pho soup boat is rich, with good seasoning and spice, and the rice-paper-wrapped fresh rolls (while probably not true to style given some of the unique ingredients) make up one of my favorite downtown lunches. Vietnamese beer is readily available, as is wine if you're not a fan of beer (say it ain't so!), along with numerous hot and iced teas such as jasmine, green, white, chrysanthemum, etc. If eating veggie is your thing, they also have a full page of options dedicated to meat-free eating.

Bernini of Ybor, 1702 E. 7th Ave., Tampa, FL 33605; (813) 248-0099; berniniofybor.com; Italian; $$$. "Why is that sculpture yelling at me?" you may ask yourself upon entering Bernini of Ybor, and the truth is, it's just an angry sculpture and it'll do you no good trying to reason with it, so go get some food and wine! Bernini is a great spot to get some Neapolitan-style pizza from the huge wood-fired oven right in the middle of the restaurant. The crust is typically lightly blackened and slightly crispy, with a bit of pull to the bread inside—pizza is definitely one of Bernini's strengths. The way to truly and fairly judge the quality of a pizza (or so the author believes) is to get a Neapolitan-style pie or a Margherita pie (named for Queen Margherita, who was visiting Naples in 1889 and saw a pizza there with tomato, buffalo mozzarella, and basil, and loved that the colors were those of the Italian flag; the rest is history) and eat it right out of the oven (as soon as it reaches sub-burn-the-roof-of-your-mouth-off temps). Is there a slight "snap" to the underside of the pie when you take a bite, or is it just limp? Is the crust and underside lightly blackened and can you smell the toasty caramelized aroma of the bread? Is there just enough salt in the dough that it opens your palate to appreciate the rest of the flavors? Is the cheese high quality, gooey, and not rubbery? Is the basil (if equipped) floral smelling, fresh, and aromatic? If you answered "yes" to all these questions, then get to eating! There is a short window after a pie like that leaves the oven where it is one of the most tremendous foodstuffs on the planet, and it usually only lasts a matter of minutes. Bernini's menu also has a host of other salads, sandwiches, pastas, and even tasty entrees such as crispy duck with goat cheese mashed potatoes and a black cherry vanilla Chianti sauce, or the pistachio-crusted grouper with herbed mashed potatoes. Yum.

The Bricks of Ybor, 1327 E. 7th Ave., Tampa, FL 33605; (813) 247-1785; thebricksybor.com; American; $$. The skateboard-loving owners of Skate Park of Tampa did something most skateboarders typically don't do—they opened a restaurant. Not only that, they opened a pretty good one too, with a quirky and eccentric menu and decor that is somewhere between "skateboarder" and "hipster," but all in good fun. The decor is (surprise!) brick-covered walls with funny and retro art on the walls along with some craft beer paraphernalia and lighter colored wood making up the bars and tables. The menu's focus is house-made product and a lot of local sourced veggies (they even have a rooftop garden where they grow a lot of what you eat!), and although there are no shortage of carnivorous options, many are very veggie-driven and make the produce the star of the show, rather than the protein. The servers are nice but very laid-back, almost to the point of being hip, and the bar is the place to sit, as you get the best service, the nicest table, and you're closest to the "sauce"!

Cafe Dufrain, 707 Harbour Post Dr., Tampa, FL 33602; (813) 275-9701; cafedufrain.com; Modern American; $$$. Even though there are fewer than a half-dozen restaurants on Harbour Island (the island is almost entirely residential), it just so happens one is among Tampa's best and most creative. Under the watchful eye of Chef Ferrell Alvarez, Cafe Dufrain conceives some absolutely fantastic creations, and the best part is that nearly all of the food is sourced locally. The restaurant offers gorgeous waterfront views of Downtown Tampa; a fantastic wine, liquor, and beer selection;

contemporary interior decor; and a friendly and knowledgeable waitstaff. Nearly every facet of Cafe Dufrain is downright sexy. Menu items may include such deliciously genius concoctions as pork cheeks with onion-bacon marmalade, coffee-rubbed brisket with spicy braised kale, or a four-hour pork Bolognese with gnocchi and ricotta. Go ahead, pretend you aren't hungry. If that didn't convince you, now imagine eating those dishes while dining al fresco with palm trees overhead and Tampa's skyline reflecting off the water in the background as the sun sets. Bon appetit.

Cafe Hey, 1540 N. Franklin Ave., Tampa, FL 33602; (813) 221-5150; cafehey.com; Sandwiches; $. There aren't too many coffee shops in the area that are almost as popular for lunch as they are for java, but Cafe Hey is certainly on that list. They may actually be the entire list, but their eclectic food keeps people coming back for more. Let's say you want a sandwich. Let's say you couldn't decide between a banh mi and a Cuban sandwich. Problem solved, Cafe Hey invented the Mi Cubano (roast mojo pork, swiss, mayo, and jalapeño/cilantro/carrot slaw on La Segunda Cuban bread). There are a number of other great sandwiches, many Asian-influenced, and numerous vegan and veggie options. Coffee is of the locally roasted variety thanks to **Buddy Brew Coffee** (p. 37) and their teas are also sourced locally from **Kaleisia Tea Lounge** (p. 80). Live music Friday nights and a very relaxed atmosphere make this a popular hangout for college students and young artists (and admittedly a hipster or two). Perhaps the only downside is that the restaurant is a little north of Downtown in an area that may seem a little sketchy to someone visiting for the first time, but don't worry; the food is worth it.

Eddie & Sam's NY Pizza, 203 E. Twiggs St., Tampa, FL 33602; (813) 229-8500; eddieandsamspizza.com; Italian; $$. It's in the watah, fuhgeddaboutit. Stepping into Eddie & Sam's NY Pizza is a lot like stepping into your typical city pizza joint in Brooklyn, only you're in downtown Tampa. The owner, a New York transplant (naturally), came to Tampa in the 1990s and wanted to share his love and knowledge of the Big Apple's pie with us so he flew down some pizzaiolos from his hometown along with a few cases of the sacred Catskill Mountain water that is said to make pizza up there so good, bought a couple ovens, and started cranking out pies. Pretty decent pies. Pizza by the slice (and these are big slices, too) with a wide variety of toppings and selections, made-to-order pizza, heros, calzones, pasta dishes, and salads are on the menu, but you don't go to a cupcake shop to buy a doughnut. Stick to the pizza if you know what's good for ya, pal.

Fly Bar and Restaurant, 1202 N. Franklin St., Tampa, FL 33602; (813) 275-5000; flybarandrestaurant.com; Tapas; $$$. In Downtown Tampa lies a bar that is more than a bar. It is actually two bars, and a restaurant to boot. Fly Bar is a great place to get a few small plates and some cocktails, and to enjoy local art in the lower level of the restaurant. If the weather is agreeable, it's an amazing place to hang out on the rooftop and enjoy the night sky and the view of Downtown, also while having cocktails, of course. Some favorites here are the truffled mac n' cheese (who doesn't like mac n' cheese?), grilled lamb tenderloin with Mediterranean accompaniments, and the scallop ceviche. Live music on weekends ensures Fly is a very lively venue, as the clientele is typically of the well-dressed and well-heeled variety. Want an insider tip? They (like many of Tampa's better restaurants) have a happy hour Sun to Fri, where one could purchase drinks and menu items at a substantially reduced price, should one be so inclined.

Fresh, 507 N. Franklin St., Tampa, FL 33602; (813) 229-5500; eatfreshdaily.com; American/Salads; $. They have a cereal bar. *Cerealously* (sorry, it was too easy), they do. You can mix and match numerous breakfast cereals and toppings (such as gummy worms!) or get some pre-made concoctions like the "Lucky" (Lucky Charms, Cinnamon Toast Crunch, and Fruity Pebbles garnished with rainbow sprinkles. Yes, it's delicious.) Yes, your kids are going to go berserk—bring an insulin needle and/or a crushed-up Tylenol PM in a doughnut or something. Fresh is much more than cereal. They have a huge array of soups, salads, and sandwiches, with more toppings and options than you could shake a stick at. It's heaven and hell—heaven for adventurous people and people who are very particular about what they want on their meal, and hell for people who are indecisive. Try not to get behind someone in line who looks like they won't even begin to try to figure out what they want prior to their turn to order; it's excruciating.

La Creperia Cafe, 1729 E. 7th Ave., Tampa, FL 33605; (813) 248-9700; lacreperiacafe.com; French; $. For such a simple food, crepes sure are a lot of fun. Ingredients range from sweet to salty, from crunchy to creamy, and combinations in-between are endless. Choose your poison and watch the crepe-technician behind the counter measure out the perfect amount of batter onto the iron before spreading it in one smooth, circular motion so the crepe cooks evenly and caramelizes just enough so that it's slightly brown and has just the tiniest bit of crispiness to it. Then he (or she) artfully adds in your choice of ingredients and folds you a pocket of deliciousness that you're ready to tear into, but wait! There's more: the gingerly sprinkled powdered sugar, the drizzle of chocolate, the sliced strawberry garnish . . . OK, maybe the French aren't so bad after all. La Creperia Cafe also has entree crepes (not just dessert) with great choices like jambalaya or pescadore, and a number of other bistro foods such as homemade soups, sandwiches, salads, and pastas, but as stated earlier, you don't go to a cupcake shop to buy a doughnut. Here, crepes are the way to go!

The Laughing Cat, 1811 N. 15th St., Tampa, FL 33605; (813) 241-2998; thelaughingcat.com; Italian/Mediterranean; $$$. Hearing the words "The Laughing Cat" doesn't necessarily immediately make one think "Hey, that sounds like a snazzy Italian restaurant!" Well, you better think again then, *paizan*, because Ybor City has a gem of an Italian restaurant called The Laughing Cat, and it's got snazzy just oozing right out of its oven. All seriousness aside, the name actually comes from one of the chef's favorite eateries in Venice, Italy, and the menu is one of the better classic Italian menus in town. Truth be told (and a lot of Italian people may be upset about this), there aren't a lot of great Italian restaurants in town. There are restaurants with great ambiance, but the food and service fall short. Canned tomato sauce, boxed pasta, cheap meatballs—these things would make your Italian grandmother cry, and

you wouldn't want to make her cry if you know what's good for you, eh? Bada-bing! On to the food! Gnocchi is a knockout, be it the tricolored gnocchi with filet mignon and mushrooms, or the sweet potato gnocchi with eggplant, 'shrooms, onions, and a basil-nutmeg sherry wine sauce. Magnifico. Seafood, veal, chicken, everything is comforting, flavorful, well seasoned, and well spiced. *Mange!*

L'Eden, 500 N. Tampa St., Tampa, FL 33602; (813) 221-4795; dine-at-leden.com; French; $$. Classic high-end French food is a cuisine that seems to be getting less and less popular over the past decade in Tampa Bay, possibly because of the painful pricing and the "prim and proper" presentation. Many local French restaurants have closed up shop or changed concept, perhaps because Floridians seem to celebrate relaxation, and having to be very conscious of one's actions throughout a meal is no longer as appealing. Fortunately, Chef Gerard Jamgotchian has thrown stuffiness right out the window. A walking library of cuisine, Jamgotchian trained in Europe, New York, California, and the Caribbean in addition to his native France, and it shows in his menu. His restaurant L'Eden is a pleasant downtown bistro that blends a number of international dishes together into a strong menu showcasing favorites from around Europe and beyond. In the mood for tapas? Order the *gambas* (shrimp with garlic) or ceviche. Maybe something more French? The ratatouille is excellent, the duck and brie crepe is decadent and unctuous, and the cheese plate is divine. There are even Indian, Russian, and Middle Eastern selections, truly something for everyone.

Samurai Blue, 1600 E. 8th Ave., Tampa, FL 33605; (813) 242-6688; samuraiblue.com; Sushi; $$$. HAI-YAH! Be careful when entering Samurai Blue in Historic Ybor City; it's said that there's a real ninja named "Blue" hiding about the sky-high ceilings, and he drops down from time to time, slapping your hand with a reed if you eat your sushi in a disrespectful manner! Well, in fairness that was said by an inebriated homeless guy outside the restaurant, and he was saying it to a cat, so you really have to take that whole story with a grain of salt. On to the food! Samurai Blue has some of the

sexier sushi around and is in a really fun space that was a cigar factory many moons ago. The sushi is pretty darn tasty but hardly authentic (if you go to Japan and ask for sushi with cream cheese or mayonnaise on it, the chef will probably throw a knife at you!), so take some friends and have a fun time. The atmosphere is geared toward enjoying yourself and having a few cocktails rather than exploring the intricacies of authentic Japanese cuisine. (Searching for a truly ethereal, authentic sushi experience? Check out **Kaisen Sushi** on p. 91).

Sea Dog Cantina, 1208 E. Kennedy Blvd., Tampa, FL 33602; (813) 280-2999; seadogcantina.com; Mexican; $$. A welcome addition to the Grand Central condo towers, Sea Dog Cantina filled a huge void in the area, and that was a decent restaurant. With hundreds (if not thousands) of apartment-dwellers inhabiting the new Grand Central condo towers, they needed a couple things, the first being somewhere to have a beer, naturally, and they hit the jackpot with Sea Dog's neighboring microbrew draft house (and wine bar), Pour House. Months later Sea Dog's doors opened, and the recipe was complete and residents were happy. The menu is loosely based around Mexican food but was designed with two things in mind: freshness and the ability to please everybody (the inhabitants of Grand Central appear to be primarily a mix of fitness models and young businesspeople). Want to indulge? Get the baked bacon jalapeño mac n' cheese. Want to behave? Go with one of their numerous salads. This is less a foodie destination than it is a place to grab a tasty bite while having an incredible craft-brewed beer next door at the Pour House (one of Tampa's best beer bars), but the food is tasty and fresh.

Shrimp & Co. Restaurant, 2202 E. 7th Ave., Tampa, FL 33605; (813) 374-0192; shrimpandco.com; Seafood; $$. Sometimes people don't give fried seafood the respect it deserves. Frying can be an art form, and given that eating fried food isn't something you ideally want to do every day, when you do eat it, you want it to be worth every delicious calorie. Apparently the owners and chefs of Shrimp & Co. know that, because everything they fry, they fry pretty spot-on, and they use as much seafood from the Florida (and surrounding) coast as possible. The cuisine has been referred to as "New Florleans" style, as it's a bit of a mix of Floridian and Cajun/Creole. There are also numerous tasty, non-fried options including crab legs, mud bugs (crawfish), spiced fish fillets, peel-and-eat shrimp, and some darn fine desserts (Key lime pie anyone?). All that being said, your safest bet may just be to come in, have a shrimp po'boy, and watch the pedestrians on the Ybor City streets walk by.

Sono Cafe, 120 W. Gasparilla Plaza, Tampa, FL 33602; (813) 274-8130; tampamuseum.org; Italian; $$. A sister restaurant to the longstanding Tampa powerhouse **Mise En Place** (p. 35), Sono Cafe at the Tampa Museum of Art offers a more simplified, ingredient-focused "slow food" menu and couples it with one of the best views of any restaurant in the city. Care for a recommendation to get the most enjoyment out of your visit to Sono Cafe? Pick a nice day, sit by the window, get some cheese, charcuterie, and a glass or three of wine, and relax. Watch the boats slip by along the river, watch the kids play in Curtis Hixon Park, enjoy all this beauty that the taxpayers ponied up the loot for, because I bet it wasn't cheap! The museum atmosphere (although visually it's strikingly beautiful) can be a bit off-putting given how quiet it is, so a table outside isn't a horrible idea either.

Sunday's Fine Dining, 1919 E. 7th Ave., Tampa, FL 33605; (813) 248-4000; sundaysfinedining.com; American; $$$. White tablecloths, wooden chairs, brick walls, modern art. Oh, and great food! Sunday's Fine Dining was a welcome addition to Tampa's Historic Ybor City district in the past months, and in the restaurant's short time occupying its cozy space at 1919 E. 7th Ave., the fare has garnered more attention than many restaurants have in years. Asian, European, and American favorites get a bit of a twist in one direction or the other, but typically for the better. Some tasty items from the menu include the "Knuckle Sandwich," which has lobster claw and knuckle meat with an Old Bay aioli, or the brick-pressed duck with anjou pear slaw. Brunch is one place that Sunday's really shines (how ironic, on Sunday!) with some mouthwatering creations like lemon ricotta pancakes with citrus butter, toasted almonds, and orange zest, or the equally impressive Sunday's Benedict, with truffled hollandaise, tomato confit, spinach, focaccia toast, and shaved Parmesan with smoked salmon.

Tampa Bay Brewing Company, 1600 E. 8th Ave., Tampa, FL 33605; (813) 247-1422; tampabaybrewingcompany.com; Pub Fare; $$. Craft beer is an underappreciated art form. So much of the USA is still sipping on mass-produced suds that were made by machines rather than hardworking Americans and that use chemicals and the cheapest ingredients available to maximize profits, rather than focus on quality and taste. The drinkable, flavorful beverages micro-brewers produce is fortunately abundantly available in Tampa Bay, which is blessed to be the area of Florida with the biggest concentration of great microbreweries. Tampa Bay Brewing Company was one of the first microbreweries in Tampa (1995) and is currently the only one in Ybor City. Their menu utilizes beer as an ingredient whenever possible, such as their jalapeño beer cheese soup, the brewhouse cider wings, or the brewhouse barleywine meat loaf with mushroom demi-glace, all of which beg the question . . . why don't more people cook with beer? Burgers are a favorite at TBBC;

one not to miss is the "Bomb," which has a half-pound burger with bacon, cheddar, fries, and onion rings, wrapped in pizza dough, and baked and finished with horseradish sauce. Sitting indoors is a fun time; the bar is a great place to learn about the brewery's different beers and chat with the bartenders, or choose a booth facing the big brewing tanks and enjoy the scenery. Fact is that 12 of their 16 tanks are right from the Bass Ale brewery in England. Outdoor seating is also fantastic, with a second bar outdoors, fans, a good bit of shade, and a great spot for conversation. Cheers!

Taps Wine and Beer Restaurant, 777 N. Ashley Dr., Tampa, FL 33602; (813) 463-1968; tapswineandbeer.com; Modern American; $$$. Taps is a fun spot. I know that sounds simplistic, but it really is a fun place to go and hang out with friends, grab a pint and a bite before heading to the museum or walking around Downtown, or maybe even on your lunch break; we won't tell! Sandwiches and small plates, dozens of microbrews on draft, and plenty of wine on tap, too (they have this neat little system where you "charge" up a card with money and go around to different wine dispensers using the card to get pours of wine). Bear in mind though, drinking wine this way isn't cheap (the draft beer prices aren't exactly cheap either), but you're also in a high-end high-rise condo building right across the street from the Tampa Museum of Art and the recently developed and stunningly beautiful Curtis Hixon Park, which abuts right up to the Hillsborough River. Location, location, location. Give the trio of dips a shot (Latin-spiced black bean with grilled pita bread? Yes, please!), and the pesto-buffalo-mozzarella bruschetta washes down with a nice IPA. Repeat as necessary.

Thai Thani, 615 Channelside Dr., Tampa, FL 33602; (813) 228-9200; thaithani.net; Thai; $$$. One usually expects to see copious amounts of gold, grandiose statues, paintings, pictures, tapestries, fountains, and more when entering a Thai restaurant. Well, don't get excited, Thai Thani is exactly like that. The benefit to Thai Thani (and this is rarely a benefit, please note the author is very much against chain restaurants) is that they have a much larger budget to work with and are in the Channelside district of Tampa, where cruise ships dock nearly year-round, filling the bars and nightclubs and (you guessed it) restaurants in the multimillion-dollar semicircle alcove that neighbors the port for these luxury liners. Thai Thani's menu is primarily classic Thai dishes, but they are well executed, service is prompt and friendly, and they will actually make food "Thai spicy" for you. One thing a non-Asian spice-addict may see frequently in Tampa is that it's hard to be taken seriously when asking for food at the maximum spicy level. Now, many of you may not desire this near-death (or is it near-enlightenment?) level of heat from your dinner, but the few who do will be grateful to have read this.

Wat Mongkolrata Temple, 5306 Palm River Rd., Tampa, FL 33619; (813) 621-1669; Thai; $. Thai Temple (technically called the Wat Mongkolrata Temple) isn't a restaurant; it's literally a place of worship. Every Sun from around 10 a.m. to 2 p.m. what appear to be monks, volunteers, and Thai grandmothers all come out to make a feast for the senses. The campus is composed of a number of different beautiful buildings, with golden roofs, Old-World classic Thai architecture, and sculptures and statues placed about, all looking over the Palm River. Picnic tables are abundant along the riverside, and people of all ages and ethnic backgrounds sit together and share the common bond of delicious food in pleasantly shaded riverside seating. The food! Dishes are very traditional indeed. The ladies making the food typically don't speak much English; your best bet is to just say "Pork!" or "Beef!" when asked what you'd like to eat. Multiple stations are set up: a couple different noodle soup stations, a fried food station, a cafeteria-style prepared foods section, and a dessert table with intricately decorated colorful desserts, most of which are very foreign-looking to the American eye. The best plan of attack here is to show up early (it gets really crowded by noon), bring friends, get someone to stand in every line, get something from each, and then meet up at a picnic table and everyone share everything family style. It's all great, and it's all fun to try!

The Columbia, 2117 E. 7th Ave., Tampa, FL 33615; (813) 248-4961; columbiarestaurant.com; Spanish; $$. The Columbia is as much a part of Ybor City as the district's famous brick roads. Owned by the Gonzmart family for generations, the restaurant has grown and grown from a small corner cafe catering to cigar factory workers in 1905 to the behemoth 1,700-seat restaurant it is today. With its hand-painted Spanish tiles, hand-carved fountains and statues, and a variety of other beautiful classical Spanish-themed elements, walking through the grandiose rooms of the Columbia is like walking from hall to hall in an art museum. The 15-page menu at The Columbia is as expansive as everything else about the restaurant, encompassing soups, salads, tapas, seafood, steak, paellas, and desserts, and their Cuban sandwich is among the better in Tampa. (A few years back the owner worked with local food historian Andrew Huse and reorganized his Cuban sandwich from the ground up, even buying a $50,000 oven just to properly cook the pork!) Few restaurants have put forth the effort to make as authentic a Cuban as The Columbia. Their sangria is a house favorite, and if you fall in love with the beautiful, hand-painted pitchers the drink is served in, don't worry, they're available for sale to go.

Malio's Prime Steakhouse, 400 N. Ashley Dr., Tampa, FL 33602; (813) 223-7746; maliosprime.com; Steak House; $$$$. The cylindrical Rivergate Tower (or, as some may call it, the "Beer

Can" building) on the Hillsborough River in Downtown Tampa is an immediately identifiable building in Tampa's skyline. It is one of the tallest limestone buildings in the world and was designed by famous architect Harry Wolf. Inside this beautiful and iconic building lies the equally beautiful restaurant Malio's, Downtown's premier steak house, with very high-end, expensive modern decor and lighting, and an equally expensive menu to boot. The menu is typical high-end steak house with large cuts of top-quality meat cooked to order over a high-temperature grill, with the usual steak sides such as spinach, mushrooms, asparagus, and mac n' cheese. If you're looking for a swanky spot to flex those expense account muscles, Malio's is the place to impress.

Specialty Stores, Markets & Producers

King Corona Cigars, 1523 E. 7th Ave., Tampa, FL 33605; (813) 241-9109; kingcoronacigars.com. Ybor City was the heart of Tampa in the late 1880s, thanks to the cigar manufacturing industry brought here from Cuba by Vicente Martinez Ybor. After King Corona successfully set up shop in Tampa, many additional cigar manufacturers followed the lead and turned the previously uninhabited patch of sandy land into a cultural hot spot of Cuban, German, Italian, and Chinese immigrants. Today, cigar factories have all but closed up, yet the passion for cigars, Cuban coffee, Cuban sandwiches, and relaxing outdoors in Ybor City "Cuban style" lives on. King Corona is one of Ybor's premier cigar shops, with espresso drinks and Cuban coffee available, a huge variety of smokes, Cuban sandwiches and other cafe snacks, even ports, wines, and beer available for sipping. If one would like the "full experience," *Guayaberas* (Cuban button-up short-sleeved shirts) and Panama hats are available for purchase, and there is a large outdoor space with tables to pull up a chair and enjoy your afternoon with a nice creamy smoke and a rich, aromatic coffee.

Kuba Cigars, 243 E. Davis Blvd., Tampa, FL 33606; (813) 258-8191; kctampa.com. Sometimes a man needs to sit down in an overstuffed leather chair, light up a cigar, turn off the phone and the TV, and just relax. Kuba Cigars, Davis Island's premier cigar shop, is a great spot to do just that. Kuba has an extensive selection of smokes in their humidor, comfortable seating, and a variety of beers too, should you be craving Tampa's own Cigar City Maduro Brown Ale to go with your Padron Maduro.

La Segunda Central Bakery, 2512 N. 15th St., Tampa, FL 33605; (813) 248-1531; lasegundabakery.com. La Segunda Central Bakery won't impress you when you drive up. It won't impress you when you walk in the door either. But once you take a bite of their warm Cuban bread fresh from the oven, you better be sitting down. Said to make the best Cuban bread in the world, La Segunda

Central sells thousands of loaves of their bread to dozens of restaurants in the Bay each day. Anyone who claims to make one of the best Cuban sandwiches in the Bay had better be making it on La Segunda bread, or locals just won't believe their claims and will likely eat somewhere else! It's that important. La Segunda also sells a number of classic Cuban pastries, makes cakes, and caters weddings, birthdays, everything under the sun, but once again, of all their talents none is greater than that perfect crispy-shelled bread with pillowy soft insides.

TeBella, 227 E. Davis Blvd., Tampa, FL 33606; (813) 254-1212; tebellatea.com. TeBella is Davis Island's own artisan tea shop. The long, narrow space is split by a bar, behind which nearly a hundred varieties of loose tea can be made into hot or iced tea drinks by owner and tea fanatic Abagail St. Clair. Need something to nosh on with your tea? TeBella offers some wonderful scones, cookies, and, best of all, French macarons made by Kim Yelvington (pastry chef of **Bern's Steakhouse** [p. 34]) that are absolutely out-of-this-world good. French macarons are an art, and there are few artists of the medium who can "wield a brush" the way Kim does. Whether you like your tea red, white, green, black, or blended, TeBella is a delightful tea shop not to miss.

Tre Amici at The Bunker, 1907 N. 19th St., Tampa, FL 33605; (813) 247-6964; yborbunker.com. Tre Amici at The Bunker is an art-riddled coffee shop staffed by good baristas and filled with great relaxing Ybor atmosphere. Live music is popular, as is encouraging discussion about how to beneficially impact the cultural, environmental, and economic aspects of the fantastic city of Tampa, as the owners are local independent small-business owners who are big supporters of growing like business and keeping community money local rather than supporting big chains.

West Palm Wines, 2009 N. 22nd St., Tampa, FL 33605; (813) 241-8587; westpalmwines.com. West Palm Wines is open for business in Historic Ybor City, selling top-notch wines Mon to Sat, but their oenophile alcove "Beaune's Wine Bar" is only open Thurs to Sat, serving up the same fantastic wines by the glass and offering "wine bar grub" to nosh on as you swirl your juice. What is wine bar grub, you ask? Goodies like artisan cheeses, charcuterie, frog legs, duck confit, *foie gras*, you name it; if it appeals to the discerning palate and pairs well with vino, Beaune's serves it up 5 p.m. to 11 p.m. If you find yourself in the Ybor City district, it's well worth stopping by.

USF, Temple Terrace & Wesley Chapel

The area surrounding universities is often a great place to find inexpensive and delicious food, especially ethnic food. The area surrounding the University of South Florida is no exception, where many no-fuss eateries exist, and a filling and tasty meal can be had on a student's budget. This is a great place to explore for food lovers in search of international treats that are much less common in other parts of Tampa, but be sure to stay on the main roads, as some areas can seem less safe than others.

Bagels Plus, 2706 E. Fletcher Ave., Tampa, FL 33612; (813) 971-9335; Bagels; $. Finding a decent bagel in Tampa is a much more daunting task than one would assume. Fortunately for you, you have this book! Those of you in search of the best bagel Tampa has to offer, head on over to the University of South Florida (USF) area and into the subtle and unassuming Bagels Plus. Transplants from New York, local bagel addicts, and students populate this artisan bagel shop, which typically sells out by lunchtime, so show up early if you want the good stuff! Many swear by the bacon and scallion bagel, but if your sweet tooth is "acting up," then the house favorite egg bagel with strawberry cream cheese may very well be the correct prescription to cure your ailment.

Chopstix, 1441 E. Fletcher Ave., Tampa, FL 33612; (813) 632-3293; tampachopstix.com; Chinese; $$. The area surrounding USF is a great place to explore a diverse variety of different foods and cultures, and it's also a great place to get a lot of food for not a lot of money (students aren't known for being the wealthiest consumers ever). Chopstix is a good place to explore authentic Chinese food (and to do so inexpensively), and it's also a great spot to gently introduce picky eaters or people who are accustomed to boring Americanized Chinese food like General Tso's chicken or lo mein and expand their palate with interesting new foodstuffs like dim sum (steamed dumplings), jellyfish, tripe, hot pots (the spicy tofu seafood hot pot is excellent), and more. Also a great spot to entertain a group on a budget, most menu items are under $10 and portions are pretty generous, but the food will be the star of the show. At this price you can't expect that the decor would be much more than "modest."

Del Rio's Cafe, 3210 N. Armenia Ave., Tampa, FL 33607; (813) 870-0217; delrioscafetampa.com; Cajun/Creole/Spanish; $$. After losing his chefing gig when Smoke (former South Tampa barbecue hot spot, now **Boca** [p. 11]) closed its doors on Platt Street, Chef Dave Del Rio saw an opportunity to open a restaurant with cuisine near and dear to his heart. A longtime Tampa resident, Del Rio loved eating a blend of Spanish, Italian, and Creole food that was common in his youth but proves difficult to find today, that is until Del Rio's Cafe opened. Menu items feature throwbacks like "bollitos" (spicy fried black-eyed-pea fritters) and *basa enchilados* with a spicy crabmeat over a mild white fish, and more popular items such as po'boys or red beans and rice with andouille sausage and warm Cuban bread. The space is as unpretentious as the menu: simple yet effective with an old Florida feel. Inexpensive, tasty, and filling, Del Rio's is a piece of history well worth eating!

Ella's Americana Folk Art Cafe, 5119 N. Nebraska Ave., Tampa, FL 33603; (813) 234-1000; ellasfolkartcafe.com; American; $$. "Eclectic" doesn't begin to describe the Seminole Heights hot spot known as Ella's Americana Folk Art Cafe. Half-buried bowling balls line the path to enter the restaurant, and after walking past the large recycled-who-knows-what-artsy-rusty sculpture of a horse, head up the stairs (note the awesome wooden porch on your right perfect for outdoor dining) and into this cafe from a time that never was. Art with intergenerational influence (everything from Elvis to license plates to robots made from cooking utensils) lines the walls, tables, windows, nearly every open square inch of the joint. The discordant decor is still very much rooted in American history though, and the menu evokes domestic (Southern) heritage, too. Appetizers range from the goofy "Fat Japs" (fried pulled pork and cream cheese–stuffed jalapeños with horseradish sauce) to the borderline elegant risotto cakes (which are fried crispy and served with goat cheese ragu and a balsamic reduction). Salads, soups, sandwiches, pizza, and burgers all follow suit, ranging from unassuming to edgy and over the top. Ella's has a great drink selection with a full liquor bar, a reasonably priced selection of wine and local craft beer, and some very entertaining bartenders to boot. The absolute best offering of Ella's is their genius brunch they affection-ately call "Soul Food Sundays." This shouldn't be a hard sell: Their Bloody Marys are served with a rib in them. Food? Sides include Southern staples such as collards, cheese grits, fried pickles, smoked corn on the cob, sweet potato salad, corn bread, and more, while larger plates get even more fun with items like the fried chicken and waffles, a half-pound alligator burger, and a host of Kansas

City–style barbecue. For dessert? Sure, banana and peanut butter chimichangas sound great, as does sweet potato pie, but few make it beyond the chocolate-covered bacon. Yes, that's a real thing.

Jai Ho Indian Cuisine, 2311 E. Fowler Ave., Tampa, FL 33612; (813) 631-8439; jaihofoods.com; Indian; $$. If you're looking for tasty Indian food at an absolute bargain, look no further than Jai Ho. Less than a mile from the University of South Florida in an unassuming strip mall (aren't they always?) sits a mom-and-pop Indian restaurant with a lunch buffet for less than $10 that will satisfy even the hungriest of appetites. Decorated with colors so bright even a blind person would take notice, this little eatery plows through the stereotype of buffets serving low-quality or less-than-yummy food. Every day the offerings change slightly, but consistently better than half of the dozen-plus items under the big stainless steel lids rank as drool-inducing, and chances are very low that diners will make it through a meal without returning for seconds, thirds, or even more. Butter chicken, curry goat, and tandoori are common selections, while there are also a number of veggie options for people who don't dig on animals. Whatever the occasion, Jai Ho is an absolute steal of a deal when it comes to lunch!

Mr. Dunderbak's, 14929 Bruce B. Downs Blvd., Tampa, FL 33613; (813) 977-4104; dunderbaks.com; German/Pub Fare; $$. Itching for some earthy, creamy, delicious Jagerschnitzel? Perhaps some brats with spicy mustard and one of over 50 draft beers? Arguably the best wurst in Tampa is at the ever-popular Mr. Dunderbak's in the Tampa Palms area, just north of the University of South Florida. Employees are easily identified by their tee shirts, which read "Beer Geek," and can also happily point you in the direction of some tasty suds, if you're not versed in the dozens of non-macro brews on draft. Should you drink your way into a newfound love affair with microbrewed beer while sitting in Dunderbak's indoor gazebo/beer garden, you're in luck: Homebrewing kits are available for purchase and you can even join their homebrewers club, which is one of the most award-winning and knowledgeable in the state. Dunderbak's also has a huge variety of goodies to go, like German candies, cookies, pressed meats and sausages, German beers, and more. A beginner's tip—don't go in asking for a "Bud Light" or anything that "tastes like a Bud Light." Even if you don't get booted out, you'll still look silly at best. Just ask a beer geek for something cold and refreshing; they're there to help!

Rana Halal Meat & Deli, 2047 E. Fowler Ave., Tampa, FL 33612; (813) 972-1550; Indian; $. Given the healthy Indian population at the University of South Florida (which is oddly enough in Central Florida, perhaps named as such because the University of Central Florida is already taken?), one would assume that naturally there would be great Indian food in the immediate vicinity. There is:

Rana Halal Meat & Deli serves up tasty and authentic Indian food in a modest (i.e., hole in the wall) setting, a mom-and-pop Indian restaurant on East Fowler Avenue that is attached to a Halal meat market. The restaurant is unlike most Indian spots in Tampa in that its cuisine is Pakistani style and dishes may be slightly less familiar to people of non-Indian descent, but the chef is quite talented at pulling off dishes like *haleem* (a barley-based slow-cooked paste that tastes much better than it looks), *nihari* (a spicy, meaty concoction that is actually the national dish of Pakistan), and *siri paya* (a Pakistani delicacy served with ginger and cilantro that includes the head and feet of a goat or lamb, *siri* meaning "head" and *paya* meaning "feet"). An adventure for the senses and the taste buds, another benefit to Rana is that it's not too much of an adventure for your wallet as the prices are reasonably low.

TacoSon, 7521 N. 56th St., Tampa, FL 33617; (813) 989-2080; tacosonmexicangrill.com; Mexican; $. TacoSon is an inexpensive, unpretentious, authentic Mexican restaurant that serves up some tasty food at a great value. Many people who love Mexican food have still never had the opportunity to try a true Mexcian delicacy— the *torta*. The *torta* is a sandwich with fluffy soft bread and the diner's choice of meat (TacoSon even has *chicharrones* in green salsa as a meat option!) with jalapeños, guacamole, refried beans, cabbage, tomatoes, and red onions, and for $5 is a pretty satisfying meal in and of itself. Another interesting and tasty Mexican specialty that can be found at TacoSon is a soup called *menudo*. Menudo is a hearty, earthy soup with a red chile base and tender slow-cooked beef tripe. It is very time-consuming to make so it's typically served only on weekends. If you put too much "salsa picante" (hot sauce) on your food, TacoSon offers a classic spiced rice milk drink that can cool even the fieriest of tongues, a great new flavor experience if you've never tried it. Beverage offerings also include fruit waters, called *aquas frescas,* and jarritos, which are Mexican fruit sodas. Mexican food in the USA has become fairly dumbed-down and Americanized with the advent of numerous chains. Finding the real deal is a very gratifying and worthwhile experience!

Tokyo Sushi Bar, 5711 E. Fowler Ave., Temple Terrace, FL 33617; (813) 983-1822; tokyosushibar.com; Japanese; $$. Some of Tampa's best sushi restaurants are small mom-and-pop spots, tucked into unassuming strip malls with minimal decoration beyond a bamboo bar and some pictures of fish on rice. Tokyo Sushi is no exception, a mom-and-pop, unimpressive decor, but darn good sushi. *Maki* (rolls) are fantastic at TS, and there are even some off-menu specialties you can ask for (tell them about the book!) such as the "CD" roll, which although by legend was named after a person, bears a striking resemblance to a compact disc. The CD roll is nearly the diameter of a woman's wrist, and attempts to eat it are not condoned by the publisher or the author, although word on the street is it's delicious. Seaweed, crab, veggies, and more stuffed into a rice-covered roll and then wrapped in sliced squid, the CD roll is in a world of its own (probably one where people have much larger mouths) and may represent more of a "challenge" than a standard menu item. Tokyo Sushi has dozens if not hundreds of choices on its menu (impressively broad given that it's a small restaurant), but the best way to order is to forego the physical menu and order fresh seasonal specialties off the markerboards hung near the sushi bar, or just ask the chef to "surprise you." This hidden gem is among the best sushi restaurants in the USF area, and far from the most expensive. If raw fish is in the cards, this may just be your ace in the hole!

Wood Fired Pizza & Wine Bar, 2822 E. Bearss Ave., Tampa, FL 33613; (813) 341-2900; wood-firedpizza.com; Pizza; $$$. The best pizza in Tampa is found at Wood Fired Pizza & Wine Bar. This is a bold claim to make and will likely upset a lot of pizza shop owners, but it is substantiated by the level of thought that goes into the pies, the meticulous detail with which they're constructed, and the elegant execution of the cooking. The owner, Peter Taylor, has achieved such a high quality of product at Wood Fired that simply referring to it as "pizza" seems almost disrespectful. Months were spent finding the perfect yeast strain, perfecting the dough recipe; nuances like salt quantity and water purification processes were tweaked time and time again. The tomato sauce is made from all San Marzano tomatoes, the mozzarella is made in house, and many of the other cheeses are made specifically for the restaurant. The oven is custom-designed and built by Peter himself, and takes only one pizza at a time as the belief is that the full attention of the pizzaiolo should be dedicated to each masterpiece as it cooks between 800 and 900 degrees next to a blend of three different

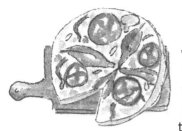

woods, chosen for their smoke-flavoring character-istics. Pizzas cook quickly; two to three minutes is the typical stay in the oven, and during cooking the pizzaiolo (cooker guy) continuously works the pie in the air to get some smokiness and blackening on the underside. Many of the herbs and vegetables are grown in nearby Plant City, Florida, specifically for the restaurant, and meat is sourced locally when possible (for example Key West pinks are the shrimp used on the "Ocean Prime"). Most of the pies at Wood Fired are unique to the restaurant and artfully imagined. Absolute knockouts include the "Dante's Inferno" (sriracha mixed with tomato sauce makes up the base for this fantastic creation, topped with slices of big meatballs, topped with a soft cheese that has the consistency of mashed potatoes and shredded Dante's cheese—possibly the best single pizza in the city) and the "Pistachio Pie" (a beautifully aromatic mixture of pistachio nuts, rosemary, fresh mozz, shaved onions, and high-quality olive oil), although it's hard to go wrong with just about any selection on the menu.

Yummy House China Bistro, 2620 E. Hillsborough Ave., Tampa, FL 33610; (813) 237-3838; yummyhousechinabistro.com; Chinese; $$. Yummy House China Bistro is Tampa's best Chinese food, hands down. The original Yummy House on Waters Avenue became so popular that the owner decided to build another and really go big. While the original restaurant was very cellular, very bland, very modest, the new Yummy House China Bistro is clean and modern, with faux painted floors, high-backed wooden chairs, white linens, and actual art on the walls! All part of his master plan, while designing and constructing his beautiful new restaurant the owner flew in chefs from San Francisco to man the kitchen so that the level of expertise behind the fryers and woks would match the aspirations for excellence he had in mind for the final concept. The 100-plus-item menu is possibly the most expansive and authentic of any Chinese restaurant in the Bay, and it has so many gems that it would take a dozen visits with a number of friends sharing to try them all. It was a dream, and he made it happen. The final product was an elegant, respectable, reasonably priced amalgamation of elements that composed the perfect Tampa Chinese restaurant. Some favorites from the menu are the salt-and-pepper calamari (which is so much more than just calamari with salt and pepper, worry not), the seafood tofu hotpot, the egg drop soup (which is elevated to a whole new level of depth and umami-richness using classic, authentic recipes rather than typical canned junk), and the XO Seafood (such a layered depth of flavors—all the XO dishes are great, but seafood is where the restaurant really shines). Bringing friends is highly recommended as most dishes (and most portions) are family style, and there are so many great selections that you'll certainly want to try more than one. Leftovers will probably happen, so here's an insider tip: liquid dishes keep (and actually develop more flavor sometimes) much better than fried foods, so if your dinner will also be tomorrow's lunch, you can plan accordingly.

Council Oak Steak & Seafood, 5223 Orient Rd., Tampa, FL 33610; (813) 627-7628; seminolehardrocktampa.com; Steak House/ Seafood; $$$$. A Las Vegas feel was what the owners had in mind for the extravagant, over-the-top temple of exquisite beef known as Council Oak Steak & Seafood, and Las Vegas is what they accomplished. Located in the Seminole Hard Rock Casino, Council Oak is easily one of the top three steak restaurants in all of Tampa Bay, and it's priced accordingly. Most appetizers range from $10 to $20, while entrees are priced from $25 to $65 and up. The beef is aged for three to four weeks to maximize concentration of flavor and texture, and if you really want to impress people at your next barbecue, uncooked steaks are even available from the Butcher Shop next door to take home. The seafood at Council Oak is impressive (the menu includes whole Maine lobster, seared diver scallops, Alaskan king crab, and more), but not having steak seems like a waste. Why go to one of the most expensive restaurants in town and order something other than their specialty? The wine list is another facet of the restaurant that got a fair amount of attention with big-name winemakers from around the globe making up the list. Although a number of bottles can be found in the $40 range, modesty once again takes a backseat to opulence. The hotel/casino is fun to visit even without a trip to the restaurant, so if a special evening is in order then dinner at Council Oak, drinks at one of the lounges, and an evening in one of the upscale hotel rooms may be

exactly what the doctor ordered, and you wouldn't have to drive anywhere (bonus!).

Skipper's Smokehouse, 910 Skipper Rd., Tampa, FL 33613; (813) 971-0666; skipperssmokehouse.com; Seafood/Cajun/Creole; $$. Fans of smoked fish (and smoked everything else) and outdoor music will have a blast at Skipper's Smokehouse. The restaurant has a fantastic outdoor stage with a lot of covered seating, and huge hundred-plus-year-old oak trees shade nearly the entire eclectically decorated outdoor area. The menu covers a good variety of seafood and has less commonly found items such as gator tail, Cajun popcorn (crawfish tails), wahoo, basa, and of course, smoked mullet. Live music fans can enjoy dinner and a show at the adjacent concert area (not huge, a modest size), and bands play at least three or four nights a week so patrons have a variety of music artists to choose from. The food is hardly gourmet, but it is tasty, and given the fun factor and the unique space, an evening at Skipper's Smokehouse will undoubtedly be an enjoyable one.

Taco Bus, 913 E. Hillsborough Ave., Tampa, FL 33603; (813) 232-5889; tampatacobus.com; Mexican/Tacos; $$. It would be difficult to find a restaurant-savvy resident of Tampa who had never heard of the Taco Bus. The cult-like phenomenon surrounding the small school-bus-turned-restaurant became so large that the owner could barely expand his operation fast enough. The 'Bus (as it's affectionately called) is open 24/7, so it quickly grew popular with college students and the after-hours crowd, along with people who work odd hours and want to grab a bite when most everything else is closed. Menu items (naturally) include tacos, and although the tacos are nothing to sneeze at, the rest of the menu is where the 'Bus really does well. *Tortas* (Mexican sandwiches) are rich and meaty, and among the tastiest things available on the menu. Veggie fans also have a number of meat-free options, with meat substitutes such as tempeh, tofu, and *rajas con queso* (roasted poblano pepper with corn and *queso fresco*). One of the best items on the menu actually has no meat: the butternut squash tostada, prepared Yucatan style with pico de gallo and *queso cotija* Mexican cheese.

Specialty Stores, Markets & Producers

Felicitous Coffee House, 11706 N. 51st St., Tampa, FL 33617; (813) 988-2828; felicitouscoffee.com. If only someone could figure out a way to keep ice cubes from watering down iced coffee. . . . Enter Felicitous Coffee, immediate neighbor to the University of South Florida and local pioneer of the frozen coffee ice cubes! Now you can let the ice in your coffee melt away, carefree, knowing that it too is made of coffee and your drink is only getting better and better. Felicitous also offers a small menu of fun bites to accompany your caffeinated beverage with clever names such as "Chai-rios," which are simply Cheerios in chai-flavored milk, or a yogurt parfait with mixed berries and granola. The shop itself is actually an old house and has a character all its own. Students are a common sighting at Felicitous given its proximity to the USF campus, but don't feel out of place if you've long since graduated—bean lovers agree it's one of the best shops in the area, and the clientele age ranges from co-ed to retiree.

Kaleisia Tea Lounge, 1441 E. Fletcher Ave., Tampa, FL 33612; (813) 977-8266; thetealounge.com. Tea aficionados, prepare to be excited. Kaleisia (a mixture of the words "kaleidoscope" and "Asia") Tea Lounge is a great place to get everything from loose-leaf tea to matcha green tea powder (known worldwide for its health benefits) to boba tea! If you've never had the opportunity to try boba tea (also known as "bubble" tea), then it's about time. Boba tea is a drink like no other, typically a milk tea served iced or as a blended iced beverage, but unique because of the "boba" tapioca pearls that sink to the bottom of the beverage and taste almost like spherically shaped gummy bears, only less chewy and less sweet (like tapioca). The tea is served with a large-diameter straw, not coincidentally the same diameter as the tapioca pearls, so that when drinking the tea through a straw, the pearls are drawn up the straw simultaneously with the liquid. It's not a concept easily conveyed with words, so get into an adventurous mood and try this fun new drink as soon as you have a chance! Kaleisia offers more than just tea and boba; they also make smoothies, chai lattes, Thai iced tea (another really interesting beverage if you've never tried it), and Vietnamese coffee. The tea shop also has a great space with couches to relax, do some work, or just enjoy your tasty drink, and free wireless, naturally.

Airport/Westshore, Carrollwood & Seminole Heights

The Westshore Business District is very close to Tampa International Airport and is home to hundreds of office buildings, along with a broad range of eateries from expensive steak houses to Mexican groceries. North of this area is Carrollwood and to the east is Seminole Heights, an up-and-coming area (read: hipsters), which has added more fun places to eat and drink month after month.

Acapulco Mexican Grocery, 1001 N. MacDill Ave., Tampa, FL 33607; (813) 873-3665; Mexican; $. *Tripa Huaraches*. Those are the only words in Spanish you should need to know when going to Acapulco Mexican Grocery, which is a hole in the wall if ever there were a hole in the wall. Aesthetically, this little grocery store isn't much to speak of. Come to think of it, the word "aesthetically" probably shouldn't even be used in the same sentence with Acapulco. Walking through the questionable-looking front door past a couple of aisles of vegetables and packaged Mexican goods will lead you to a half dozen tables set next to a deli counter and a small kitchen manned by Mexican women. Coolers line the wall, and beverage selections range from cold *cervezas* (they have a great selection of Mexican beers) to *aguas frescas* (fruit waters), and should you be in a completely insane, self-destructive sort of mood, they even carry Four Loko (which I swear was taken off the market a long time ago, but I'll just keep my mouth shut). Just grab a drink and pop it open; table service is pretty limited. Soda lovers will appreciate the classic glass bottles of Mexican Coca-Cola, which is said to taste much better due to the use of cane sugar in the Mexican version instead of high-fructose corn syrup, which sweetens the domestic version. The *Huaraches*? They're essentially corn tortillas about 6 inches in diameter that are stuffed with a thin layer of refried beans and topped with cilantro, onion, *queso fresco* (crumbly Mexican cheese), and your choice of meats. *Tripa* is in fact tripe, but don't let that dissuade you: It's absolutely one of the most delicious (and truly authentic) meats available in Mexican cuisine. Tacos at Acapulco are also delicious, but the *huaraches* are really where the magic is, and *tripa* isn't the only meat available—diners can choose from *lengua* (tongue, which is also delicious), *buche* (sweetbreads), *al pastor* (pork and pineapple), and the obligatory chicken/beef/pork. At less than $2 per taco, this little hidden gem of an eatery can satisfy any appetite and do so working within any budget!

Boizao, 4606 W. Boy Scout Blvd., Tampa, FL 33607; (813) 286-7100; boizao.com; Brazilian; $$$$. Vegans, move along, nothing to see here. Carnivores, I present to you: heaven. Boizao (which translates to "big bull" in Portuguese) is a sexy-classy Brazilian *churrascaria* (pronounced "shoo-ha-ska-ria") that has been filling tummies in Tampa since opening in 2007. Snazzily dressed servers (most of whom are genuine Brazilians) walk about the restaurant, each with a large knife and a metal skewer loaded with one of sixteen varieties of meat ready to cut off a slice or three for you. Yes, you read that correctly, Boizao offers sixteen different succulent selections of meaty goodness to choose from, everything from bacon-wrapped filet mignon to lamb chops to pork sausages and more. A substantial salad and veggie bar take up the center of the restaurant, but only suckers fill up on that stuff; your goal here should be to eat your body weight in USDA prime beef. Many people agree though that the *picanha* is the best thing on the menu—sea-salted top sirloin broiled on a spit. Yes, please! Upon being seated, each diner is given a paper disc approximately the size of a drink coaster (no, it's not a drink coaster) that is colored red on one side and green on the other, green meaning "feed me" and red meaning "I'm ready to burst." If an adult beverage is what the doctor ordered, try Boizao's Caipirinha (it's like a mojito on steroids, made with lime, sugar, and a Brazilian sugarcane liquor called Cachaca that will put hair on even the most hairless of chests). Seriously, it's like lighter fluid. An insider tip: Lunch at Boizao is less than half the price of dinner, and it's nearly the exact same meal. Just make sure you don't have anything planned for the afternoon (other than perhaps a nap-coma); that much meat will wear you out pretty quick.

Burger Monger, 10412 N. Dale Mabry Hwy., Tampa, FL 33618; (813) 968-6860; burgermonger.com; Burgers; $. A hamburger is an art form. Each component of a hamburger should be delicious on its own, and when working in harmony, all components of a great hamburger should sing a symphony of juicy awesomeness that delights with every bite. After that intro you're probably expecting a life-changing beef-on-bun experience, but it's unlikely that's what you'll find at Burger Monger. Truthfully they just make a darn good hamburger. The beef? A breed of cattle previously only found in Japan called "Akaushi" that is hormone free and said to have higher concentrations of monounsaturated (good) fats and heart-healthy acids. The buns? Garlic-buttered challah, baked fresh for the restaurant. The fries? Hand-cut, top-quality Idaho potatoes, seasoned with sea salt. Toppings, veggies, cheeses are all good-quality products, and with options like this you'll say goodbye forever to those national chain fast-food "hamburgers" with low-grade beef and who-knows-what kind of hormones and chemicals within. Yuck. Burger Monger filled a need in Carrollwood: a high-quality burger place without the high-end price tag.

Cappy's Pizzeria, 4910 N. Florida Ave., Tampa, FL 33603; (813) 238-1516; Pizza; $$. See description for Cappy's South Tampa location, p. 13.

China Yuan, 8502 N. Armenia Ave., Tampa, FL 33604; (813) 936-7388; chinayuanrestaurant.com; Chinese; $$. Chinese food is so much more than General Tso's chicken and lo mein. Nothing against either dish, but once you ditch the menu that the restaurant makes for the Americans and start choosing dishes off the menu for the Chinese people, you might never go back. You might actually never want any Chinese dish available at a shopping mall ever again once you break into the fun stuff! China Yuan is one of a few really fantastic and authentic Chinese restaurants in the Tampa Bay area, and one of the few left that has live seafood in tanks lining the wall of the restaurant. Yep, it's that fresh; you can go pick your dinner executioner-style and have some tasty seafood that was swimming just minutes prior to being cooked up. Other than the tanks, the decor at China Yuan is relatively modest, a step above fast food but hardly a place you'd take a business client (unless said client is a real food lover; in that case take them by all means!), and service is friendly but very relaxed (don't expect a sense of urgency in any of the waitstaff). China Yuan does a great job with a number of dishes, including salt-and-pepper calamari, soy sauce duck wings, and crispy taro duck. You also pretty much can't go wrong ordering anything in their black bean sauce; it has such a hearty depth of flavor that meat almost isn't necessary—but it sure is tasty.

Front Porch Grille & Bar, 5924 N. Florida Ave., Tampa, FL 33604; (813) 237-5511; frontporchgrill.com; American/Sandwiches; $$. Funky and eclectic is a recurring theme in many of Seminole Heights's hot spots, and the Front Porch Grille is no exception. Menu options are fun and unique to the restaurant (albeit not quite as off-the-wall unique as neighboring restaurant **The Refinery** [p. 99]) and range from the tame (The "Plain Ole Steak" seasoned with kosher salt and fresh ground pepper) to the more intricate (mussels *meunière* sautéed in garlic and white wine, with tomato, parsley, and French baguette for dipping). They have excellent beer selections (everything from simple domestic lagers to flavorful stouts and Belgian ales). Given that the restaurant was for many years a house, it maintains a fun, homey feel, and the large wraparound porch is a great place to dine al fresco in the more temperate months. Front Porch has live music weekly along with karaoke and a great happy hour with drink and menu specials from 4 to 7 p.m. every day. It's not a bad spot to down some wings with a few of Tampa's own Cigar City Brewing IPAs while watching the game.

Holy Hog BBQ, 3501 N. Armenia Ave., Tampa, FL 33607; (813) 879-4647; holyhogbbq.com; Barbecue; $$. True barbecue fans in Tampa Bay know the name Holy Hog, and know it well. Danny Hernandez, owner of **Pipo's Latin Cafe** (p. 117), always had a soft spot for excellent 'cue, and fortunately for the city of Tampa he decided to share his love of smoked meats with everyone when he opened up Holy Hog BBQ on Armenia Avenue. The restaurant became so popular and successful that Danny recently opened a second location in South Tampa, too, which made fans residing south of Kennedy Boulevard elated that they no longer had to drive far to get to Danny's meat. Ribs, chicken, pork sausage, and burnt ends are all moist and flavorful, but the pulled pork is thought by many to be the best thing on the menu. Brisket is very flavorful, but has been both moist and bone dry on different visits, so the pulled pork is the most highly recommended menu item. While many barbecue joints focus only on the meat and put little effort into the sides, Holy Hog does a fantastic job with collards, corn fritters (the corn fritters are amazing), mac n' cheese, fried okra, bacon corn bread, and more. Both mustard- and ketchup-based sauces are available and are house blends, although the meat needs no sauce for the most part. For some of the best 'cue in the Bay, swing by Holy Hog BBQ, and bring your appetite!

Hot Rods BBQ and Grille, 18430 Livingston Ave., Lutz, FL 33559; (813) 948-7988; hotrodsbbqgrill.com; Barbecue; $$. In the mood for something you've probably never eaten before? How about barbecued bat? If Ozzy Osbourne were a country music singer . . . Barbecued bat may be the most "interesting" item on Hot Rod's menu, but don't let that sway your decision; this off-the-wall 'cue joint really makes some excellent smoked meats. The bat (since you're still wondering about that one) is legitimately a bat (many think it's quail, as it has similar size, flavor, and texture to quail); it's a farm-raised fruit bat that Hot Rods roasts until golden brown and delightfully moist and tender—it actually tastes quite good! Conveniently located smack-dab in the middle of nowhere, Hot Rods is certainly a local's spot given that it is one of very few restaurants in proximity to the surrounding neighborhoods, but people also drive from afar to get a fix of their excellent food. The restaurant is decorated . . . well, perhaps decorated is the wrong word. Nearly every square inch of the walls inside is covered in the most oddball Southern–inspired novelties and relics. It's as if one were stepping inside an episode of *Hoarders* where the subject was an eccentric, mildly insane relative of Jed Clampett. Seriously, there's everything from a hundred-year-old telephone to a Yoda scarecrow. Yes, Yoda from *Star Wars*. Menu items are equally kooky, with selections such as the "BBQ Split," a play on a banana split, with pickles instead of bananas and scoops of pulled pork, corn bread casserole, and coleslaw replacing traditional ice cream scoops, and the obligatory bing cherry atop the masterpiece. Not that it needs additional selling, but all this edible hilarity will only set you back a paltry

$5. When looking for a humorous yet satisfying barbecue meal that won't hurt the wallet, and you just happen to be in the middle of nowhere (East Lutz), pop on in to Hot Rods—it won't disappoint.

I Ai Sushi, 3691 W. Waters Ave., Tampa, FL 33614; (813) 932-1111; Japanese/Sushi; $$. Japanese street food isn't commonly found in Tampa; sadly, Japanese food isn't well represented in Tampa at all. This is probably true because the Japanese population in Tampa is small relative to other ethnicities; you can't throw a rock without hitting a Latin or Italian restaurant these days, but Japanese restaurants where they aren't building volcanoes out of onion rings and catching shrimp tails in their toques are pretty sparse. Fortunately, I Ai Sushi on Waters Avenue is a refreshing example of how great Japanese food can be, especially given their very modest price point. Udon noodles, ramen noodles, squid salad, even omusubi rice balls are available in flavors like plum and salmon. Sushi on the other hand is less adventurous but still tasty and an excellent value, with many rolls priced under $5. I Ai (pronounced "eye-eye," which translates to "I love," so the restaurant's name is technically "I Love Sushi," those clever Japanese guys) will even prepare you a traditional Japanese New Year's Day hangover meal (if you call ahead) called *Ikura Uni Don*, which is essentially a big bowl of salmon caviar and uni (sea urchin caviar) over rice, just dripping with rich caviar goodness. It can be a bit heavy though, so bring a friend to share.

The Independent, 5016 N. Florida Ave., Tampa, FL 33603; (813) 341-4883; independenttampa.com; Pub Fare/Sandwiches/ Vegetarian; $$. The Independent (or "The Indy," as the regulars call it) is a craft beer bar in the Seminole Heights neighborhood and is pretty much the neighborhood bar for local residents. Recently the owners added a kitchen and menu featuring upscale pub grub with a number of dishes that function as excellent complements to that cold, refreshing, flavorful microbrew you're sipping on. Menu highlights include the Gouda and spiced pear grilled cheese on rye, numerous bratwurst, Bavarian pretzels, a fantastic caprese panini on local Cuban bread with house-made pesto, and The Rob (thinly sliced roast beef with horse-radish sauce on a Kummelweck bun topped with caraway seeds and kosher salt—yum). The beer selection is extensive, and dozens of microbrews with a wide variety of styles are available; your friendly bartender should be able to help you choose a glass of suds to pair with your tasty meal.

Kaisen Sushi, 14841 N. Dale Mabry Hwy., Tampa, FL 33618; (813) 969-3848; kaisensushitampa.com; Japanese/Sushi; $$$. Kaisen Sushi is unquestionably the best sushi in Tampa. That is a bold claim, but accurate: The word "kaisen" is the Japanese term meaning "continual improvement" and essentially describes a goal of continuously striving to achieve perfection. The chefs at Kaisen Sushi on North Dale Mabry Highway in Carrollwood seem to be working hard to continuously do just that. Given that it's in a strip mall (noticing a trend yet?) next to a number of other unspectacular restaurants, Kaisen doesn't look like much from the outside, and the interior decor is also quite modest but clean: white walls with a few Japanese paintings, wooden tables, and a long sushi bar make up the dining room. The true art at this unassuming sushi restaurant is what shows up on your table: only the freshest fish available is served, and great attention to detail is found in nearly every dish. Naturally, given that 99 percent of Americans aren't familiar with traditional or authentic Japanese food (no, no self-respecting Japanese person would eat a cream-cheese-stuffed fried chicken roll covered in mayonnaise, even if they could stop laughing at it), Kaisen has the obligatory domesti-cated maki rolls (which admit-tedly they do a great job with), but where the restaurant really gets creative is when a diner comes in and says the word "*omakase.*" *Omakase* is a Japanese term that means "I'll leave it to you," essentially telling the chef to make whatever he feels like creating, using the freshest fish and ingredients he has to offer. This, my friends, is where you take the sushi training wheels off and become an adult. Dishes could literally be anything the chef creates in his mind, but may include items like a tuna-seaweed salad, spicy plum marinated snapper, riceless salmon and lemon caper rolled maki, shiso masago ginger mackerel nigiri, and the list goes on. One of the most attractive aspects of ordering *omakase* at Kaisen is the value the diner gets: the customer specifies what they would like to spend ($20 to $30 per person is typically more than enough to fill you up), and the chef begins making small plates of delicious, fresh, unique seafood, staying within the budget. Kaisen Sushi creates artful and consistently excellent meals for diners, and those willing to let the chefs show them their true talent are really in for an adventure in flavors and textures that is unmatched in the Bay area.

La Cabana Antioquena, 8303 N. Armenia Ave., Tampa, FL 33604; (813) 936-0078; lacabanaantioquena.com; Colombian/ Latin American; $$. Huge portions and modest prices are a recipe for success at La Cabana Antioquena. The star of the show at this wonderful little Colombian restaurant is unquestionably the rotisserie chicken, which marinates for three days before spending three hours in a charcoal rotisserie for stunningly moist, flavorful chicken. At $8 for an entire chicken, it's not a bad deal either, and one bird will usually feed at least two people! While La Cabana specializes in chicken, they also do a great job with a number of other Colombian dishes such as *chicharrones* (fried sliced pork belly), black sausage and pork rinds, or even something as simple as red beans and rice. For a tasty authentic Colombian meal at a crazy value, La Cabana Antioquena is a perfect choice.

La Teresita Cafeteria, 3248 W. Columbus Dr., Tampa, FL 33607; (813) 879-9704; lateresitarestaurant.com; Cuban/Latin American; $.

Whole Foods Market

Whole Foods has a store in Tampa, and as with all of the outlets in this national chain, the Tampa store offers a fantastic selection of artisan cheeses, wine, microbrewed beers, baked goods, meat and fish, you name it. It's foodie paradise in there and a popular spot for lunch. There's a hot bar, cold bar, sushi, and just about any other tasty thing you could desire, along with a nice section of tables to sit at. Truffled salt? Check. Local craft beer? Check. Organic produce? Check. Another great reason to choose Whole Foods is the meat selection. All of the meat the store sells has been ethically raised and is hormone and antibiotic free, and if this sounds like marketing gibberish, please, take an hour to watch one of the many movies showing what the mass-production cattle/chicken/etc. farms do to the animals that later become your food. It'll quickly give you an appreciation for eating better-quality meat! The store is clean, the staff is helpful and friendly, and as a food lover it's hard to go in there without wanting to get one of everything! The prices on beer and wine are super reasonable too, often lower than many other stores in the area, and the selection is also among the best around. Vegaphiles will be happy to know that the store makes finding meatless options much easier, and numerous vegetarian and vegan selections are available on both the hot and cold bar. *Whole Foods Market, 1548 N. Dale Mabry Hwy., Tampa, FL 33607; (813) 874-9435; wholefoodsmarket.com/stores/tampa.*

Don't show up at La Teresita Cafeteria without your appetite, but worry not, you needn't bring much more than the change in your couch cushions to fill your belly with tasty Cuban food! One of the best bargains for food in the area, La Teresita Cafeteria is known by many to have fed entire families for less than the price of an entree at most restaurants. Latin and Cuban favorites are served (24 hours a day on weekends) in this more modest of the Capedevila family's eateries (the family's table service restaurant **La Teresita** [p. 93] is more of a traditional sit-down spot), and the place is frequented by people young and old, of all shapes, sizes, and ethnic backgrounds. Popular menu items include *puerco asado* (roast pork), *ropa vieja* (shredded beef), and *pollo asado* (baked chicken), and all are best accompanied by yellow rice and black beans, and maybe a few plantains for good measure. Whether it's used to cure a hangover, feed a poor college student, or just fill an extra-hungry tummy, La Teresita Cafeteria's grub makes a cheap, tasty, and effective meal.

Mekenita Mexican Grille, 17623 N. Dale Mabry Hwy., Lutz, FL 33548; (813) 264-1212; mekenitamexicangrille.com; Mexican; $$. Pacific-Mexican cuisine at Mekenita Mexican Grille is a favorite of many of North Tampa's residents. The owner/founder was a former decade-plus veteran chef at a national chain restaurant who decided he wanted to create a restaurant that would offer his twist on Mexican cuisine at an approachable price point, and Mekenita was born. Actually, Mariposa was born (the original name was Mariposa), but the restaurant later changed its name to Mekenita, perhaps given Mariposa's alternate meaning (it's a slang insult in certain Spanish dialects, although the literal translation is "butterfly"). The interior of the restaurant is attractively decorated, lights and lamps are artsy and colorful, and bright blue potted plants offset the earth-toned terra-cotta walls. It's almost a sit-down, table-service restaurant, but ordering still takes place at the counter and seating is per the diner's discretion. Authentic Mexican drinks like *horchata* (spiced rice milk) and *aguas frescas* (fruit waters) are available, along with a number of Spanish and Mexican beers, and sangria for those not in the mood for some suds. Menu items mix sweet, salty, tangy, and rich ingredients to achieve big flavor, such as citrus grilled chicken and pineapple plantain nachos with serrano passion fruit sour cream, or Oaxaca-style smoked pork tamales with mole negro and cilantro. Should you find yourself in the North Tampa/Lutz area and hankering for some Mexican food, Mekenita should fit the bill perfectly.

Mi Pueblo Cafeteria, 1910 N. Lincoln Ave., Tampa, FL 33607; (813) 351-0011; Puerto Rican; $. Puerto Rican cuisine is full of flavor and excitement. Mi Pueblo Cafeteria on Spruce Street and Lincoln Avenue offers a number of Puerto Rican favorites such as *jibarito* sandwiches (smashed plantains in place of bread, palomilla steak, lettuce, and an addictive garlic aji sauce), blood pudding sausage (it may sound strange but it is fantastic), *mofongo*, yucca, and more. The restaurant has a cafeteria feel, not too much in the way of decor to speak of; many of the dishes are made daily and set behind glass in warmers, and can be ordered a la carte. If you've never tried Puerto Rican food, this is an excellent place to start. The restaurant is family owned, and many recipes are probably handed down through generations, reflecting a vibrant culture and a unique and interesting cuisine.

Michael's Grille, 11720 N. Dale Mabry Hwy., Tampa, FL 33618; (813) 964-8334; michaelsgrill.com; American; $$$. Great steaks, great service, and a comfortable atmosphere make Michael's Grille a good selection for anyone looking for a nice meal in the Carrollwood area. The menu focuses on tried-and-true American and European dishes with Chef Michael's twists ramping up the flavors, and everything typically comes out perfectly prepared and attractively plated. Menu items like the Red, White, and You (three layers of red sauce, wine, and cream sauce with shrimp and crab meat) or the velvety and unctuous filet au poivre (twin pepper-crusted filets flamed in cognac with a peppercorn sauce) are where Michael's shines, but less rich (and still tasty) options are available, too. The Strawberry Fields salad features a tender blackened salmon fillet atop greens with caramelized onions, pineapple, apples, almonds, and strawberry vinaigrette. Entrees are reasonably priced; most fall in the $15-to-$20 range and peak out around $25. Wine selections are good, but many wine nuts stop in at Jenn's Wine Shop right next door to Michael's and enjoy a bottle right there at the wine bar (Michael's delivers next door), or take a bottle over to Michael's to enjoy with their meal.

Pho An Hoa, 2730 W. Waters Ave., Tampa, FL 33614; (813) 490-9157; Vietnamese; $$. Beef lovers, be excited. Pho An Hoa is a simple Vietnamese restaurant in a small strip mall that serves what many consider to be the best pho in Tampa. If you aren't familiar with pho, that's an absolute shame, so put this beefy spiced boat of fantastic soup at the top of your priorities list; it's a meal that you may very well fall head over heels in love with and begin to crave on a monthly/weekly/daily/hourly basis. Imagine a big bowl of rich beefy broth spiced with star anise and cinnamon. Now add in noodles, some fish sauce, a dab of sweet hoisin sauce, and a liberal blob of sriracha (spicy chili sauce). Slice meat and add to the warm liquid: traditional pho has steak, tendon, tripe, and meatballs, but versions with chicken, pork, or tofu are also common. Wait, it gets better: add lime juice, sweet basil, cilantro, bean sprouts, and chili peppers (or jalapeños). Stir, eat, swoon. Pho is one of the most fantastic soups on planet Earth, and Pho An Hoa makes a darn fine bowl of it. Another real treat the restaurant executes well is a higher-end meal typically served at weddings or celebrations called "bo 7 mon," which translates to "seven courses of beef." This meal should be ordered in advance and shared with friends; the flavor of each of the very different preparations in the seven courses is as much fun to discuss as it is to eat. Pho An Hoa is an absolute gem of a restaurant hidden in plain sight; it's a pity more people aren't familiar with it.

The Refinery, 5137 N. Florida Ave., Tampa, FL 33603; (813) 237-2000; thetamparefinery.com; American; $$$. "Good food is wasted on people who can afford it," thought Greg Baker while working at a high-end French restaurant two decades ago. Today he owns (with wife Michelle) the Seminole Heights staple known as The Refinery. Pioneers of the Eat Local movement in Tampa, the Bakers source everything possible from farms in the Bay area, and they are big proponents of supporting local businesses, farmers, bakers, and everything in between. The hip and recently gentrified (i.e., hipster-laden) neighborhood of Seminole Heights immediately welcomed the addition of The Refinery in 2010 and has supported the restaurant since day one, although two James Beard Award nominations for the restaurant have brought nationwide awareness to the concept and quality of the cuisine. Even world-famous chef and restaurateur Mario Batali stopped in on his last visit to Tampa to see what all the excitement was about. The restaurant is an old home that was converted to a dining establishment years prior, and given the amount of effort and additional cost the restaurant expends in order to use local and sustainable ingredients, the price points on the menu are a bargain, and the creativity of the dishes (which change every week with a new menu) has few rivals in the Bay, and even fewer if any in the immediate vicinity. Given that the menu is ever-changing, listing dishes is almost a tease but may shed light on their creative nature so here goes: egg yolk fudge (bacon tomato confit, cinnamon-morita toast, red onion herb salad, and kewpie-mustard powder), *Chiang Mai Bahhh* (pork and lamb Chiang Mai sausage, smoked eggplant, sweet chili vinaigrette, sticky rice), or the breakfast sandwich (brined, breaded, fried chicken breast, fried egg, and country gravy). Sweet treats are an adventure at The Refinery too, with goodies like lavender smoked peppercorn pound cake (sweet corn sabayon and bacon-honey gastrique) or chocolate salad (chai poached apple, 3 chocolates, cocoa cranberries, citrus gastrique). Although these exact items likely won't appear on the menu during your visit, the same level of eclectic creativity will govern the available selections. Well, that and whatever is fresh, seasonal, and available with regard to produce and proteins.

Saigon Deli, 3692 W. Waters Ave., Tampa, FL 33614; (813) 932-0300; Vietnamese; $. There is a spot in Tampa to get an impressively good sandwich for $3. Saigon Deli has been serving up its *banh mi* sandwiches to customers for years in an unassuming strip mall (get used to the strip mall thing—most of Tampa's hidden gems are tucked away in a nondescript strip mall somewhere; very few are standalone buildings). What is a *banh mi* sandwich? The term *banh mi* actually refers to the type of bread used, a French baguette (a remnant of the French colonial period in Vietnam), although in the USA the term typically refers to the full sandwich. Although the ingredients in a typical *banh mi* are cilantro, jalapeños, cucumber, shredded pickled daikon and carrot, and meaty porky goodness in the form of sweet barbecue pork, pâté, steamed pork roll, and ham, many versions in the states use a single meat or a combination of a few of them. One of the most popular *banh mis* at Saigon Deli is the sweet barbecue pork, which is not a surprise. A crispy baguette gives way to the soft bread in the interior and such a fantastically sweet and salty umami-esque presence from the pork that is offset by the clean bite of the pickled carrot and daikon shreds, accented by the herbal quality of the cilantro with a fiery finish from the jalapeños. There are few sandwiches as dynamic and layered with flavor as the *banh mi*, and perhaps none of which comes in at the absurdly low price of $3! Saigon Deli also offers numerous noodle soups, such as a nice hearty beefy bowl of pho, or the equally tasty vermicelli noodles. The flavors are fantastic, and the prices are tough to beat.

Sa Ri One, 3940 W. Cypress St., Tampa, FL 33607; (813) 874-2911; Korean; $$. Dining at a Korean restaurant is a bit different from dining at most other Asian eateries. Upon sitting (or immediately after ordering), diners are traditionally served small portions of side dishes called *banchan* in little bowls that are great for munching on right away if very hungry, or also for pairing with the main course. Traditionally the number of *banchan* would reflect the caliber of restaurant when dining out (more is better), or if dining as a guest in someone's home, the host would show great honor to the guest by bringing out numerous *banchan*. Sa Ri One is a great Korean spot in what appears to have been a home at one time that has since been converted into a restaurant. *Bi bim bap* is a very popular Korean dish Sa Ri One does well—rice is heated in a stone bowl and covered with seasoned and sautéed veggies (carrots, mushrooms, greens) and chili paste, and then topped with a fried egg. Typically upon being served the *bi bim bap*, the diner mixes everything in the bowl together using chopsticks and then enjoys layer upon layer of flavor in each bite. *Gal bi* and *bul go gi* are two more very popular dishes that the restaurant excels at—both are delightfully smoky and sweet barbecued meats (*gal bi* is short ribs and *bul go gi* is sliced beef), and both are quite addictive.

Terra Sur Cafe, 5358 W. Village Dr., Tampa, FL 33624; (813) 269-2694; terrasurcafe.com; Peruvian/Tapas; $$$. Food lovers looking for excellent tapas and top-notch Peruvian cuisine need look no further than Terra Sur Cafe. Translated "Land of the Sun," Terra Sur is decorated in earth-toned colors with racks upon racks of wine bottles on the walls. Once again, one of Tampa's best restaurants is hidden away in a nondescript shopping plaza, with thousands of people driving by each day completely unaware of the deliciousness they're passing (fortunately you got this book and you won't be missing out on this gem!). Friendly servers will happily help guide you through the menu, which is very seafood-centric but also offers a number of tasty chicken and steak dishes. Not trying at least one of the ceviches (they offer five or six different varieties on the menu) would be a sin, and by far one of the most popular menu selections to share with the table is the ceviche sampler (a plate with a generous portion of four different ceviches, which would also make a perfect main course for any seafood lover). The restaurant also features specials that may appeal to more adventurous diners, such as roasted duck hearts and grilled octopus medallions, and being adventurous is highly recommended while at Terra Sur. Let the kitchen show you what it's capable of, and you'll be rewarded with some of the tastiest food around.

Thai Terrace, 2055 N. Dale Mabry Hwy., Tampa, FL 33607; (813) 877-8955; thaiterrace.net; Thai; $$. Tampa is blessed with a number of excellent ethnic restaurants, many of which offer great food at a considerable value. A stone's throw from Tampa International Airport, the Westshore business district, and the Tampa Bay Buccaneers stadium sits a mom-and-pop Thai restaurant named Thai Terrace that is both a bargain and a delight to the senses. Noodles are a particular strength at Thai Terrace: The *pad see ew* is particularly flavorful with thick, wide rice noodles stir-fried in a peppery black soy sauce and mixed with veggies like broccoli, baby corn, and straw mushrooms. It's a dish with a particularly enjoyable contrast of flavors and textures from crunchy to soft, and from salty to sweet to rich to spicy (dishes can be tailored to your preferred heat level, ranging from mild to napalm). Decor is gilded, colorful, and opulent, as is commonly seen in Thai restaurants, with pictures of the royal family, statues of gods, and bright fabric strategically placed throughout the room. Another great selection is the sweet chili lemongrass glazed "terrace" with seafood (choose between grouper, snapper, softshell crab, and prawns). The sauce is made by cooking kaffir lime leaves, lemongrass, palm sugar, and ground bell peppers and finished with fried basil leaves, and the dish packs a flavor wallop that transitions from sweet to sour to salty with a little crunch at the end. Given the amount of love and attention each dish gets, and the very reasonable portions, Thai Terrace is a great value with most of the dishes ranging between $9 and $15. Bring friends and try as many as possible!

Udipi Cafe, 14422 N. Dale Mabry Hwy., Tampa, FL 33618; (813) 962-7300; udipiusa.net; Indian; $$. No animals were harmed in the making of Udipi Cafe, the all-vegetarian South Indian restaurant in the heart of Carrollwood. A restaurant that serves no meat seems odd to most Westerners, but Udipi still manages to have an extensive menu of South Indian dishes with a host of spices, seasonings, and exotic flavors, and all without a single piece of meat. To clarify the difference between South and North Indian food, North Indian frequently has meat and uses a lot of yogurt and cream, along with bread such as naan or paratha. South Indian food is typically vegetarian and served with rice, tends to be on the spicier side, and uses coconut as a common ingredient. When visiting Udipi, bringing dining buddies is highly recommended, as there are so many great selections on the menu that it would be hard to get a good feel for what the restaurant is capable of without either stuffing yourself or taking home a lot of leftovers! A popular menu item at Udipi is the *dosai*, a paper-thin rice crepe that can be stuffed with anything from onions and potatoes to chutney, and goes down quite well with a glass of mango juice or Indian spiced tea. Other great choices include the *baigan bartha* (baked eggplant

mashed with tomatoes and onions), *uthappam* (pancakes with onions, tomatoes, chilis, carrots, peas, and more), or *mumbai pau-bhaji* (masala veggies blended with cheese and cashews). When you walk into an Indian restaurant and you're the only one in there who isn't Indian, it usually means you've found a good spot!

Vizcaya Restaurante & Tapas Bar, 10905 N. Dale Mabry Hwy., Tampa, FL 33618; (813) 968-7400; vizcayarestaurante.com; Spanish/Tapas; $$$. Chef Felix Piedra of Vizcaya Restaurante & Tapas Bar is a character. A classically trained chef with an absolute love for food, Chef Felix is a presence in his restaurant as much as he is in the kitchen. Diners love to visit just to chat with the man, who often moves between the kitchen and dining room happily recommending dishes and telling you about the week's specials. Then he heads back into the kitchen to craft the dish for you. Chef Felix is an impressive guy—he doesn't just cook food in the style of the Basque region of Spain; he is from the Basque region of Spain, and he frequently returns for inspiration and to continue to bring back great recipes and dishes to share with diners who visit his Carrollwood restaurant. The menu has numerous excellent dishes; favorites include the *pulpo gallega* (fork-tender octopus with saffron and sea salt), the ceviche mixto (salmon, scallops, and oysters in a cilantro-lime concoction that really accents the smooth, tender seafood and gives a clean finish), and the *datiles con panceta* (an absurdly addictive combination of manchego cheese and Serrano ham stuffed in dates, then wrapped with bacon and fried, covered in a honey aioli). Vizcaya is a fantastic spot to explore the flavors of Spain. If a plane ticket to Espana is a little more than you're looking to spend, a drive to Carrollwood should be comparatively cheap.

Landmarks

Armani's, 2900 Bayport Dr., Tampa, FL 33607; (813) 207-6800; hyatt.com/gallery/tparw_armanis; Italian; $$$$. One of the most beautiful views in all of Tampa is that of sunset from the 14th floor of the Grand Hyatt Hotel, at their high-end Italian masterpiece, Armani's. Diners can enjoy a fantastic bottle of wine (their wine selection is superb, albeit expensive) and a romantic view of the sun setting over Tampa Bay (the hotel is situated right on the Bay very near the Tampa International Airport) while noshing on some of the best fine-dining Italian food around. Armani's is the perfect spot to impress someone, be it a date, a business client, the pope; nearly everyone who sets foot in that gorgeous temple of extravagant dining should leave as impressed with the space as they were with the food. Speaking of the food, the restaurant has one of the best antipasto bars in the city. It'd be a shame not to sample just a few of the offerings prior to ordering *primi piatti* (first plates). It's hard to go wrong with any of the first plates, but the *cannelloni di maiale* (stuffed with ground veal, spinach, ricotta, parm, and a silky tomato cream sauce) and the *asparagi alla milanese* (asparagus with truffled fried duck egg and Parmesan cheese) are two particularly tasty choices. Main plates are hearty and filling, and the veal dishes are highly recommended. Armani's really has elevated its osso bucco and scalloppini to be two of the finest plates around. Although a special occasion isn't necessary, there may not be a restaurant around that can beat the menu, decor, service, food, and that spectacular view—don't dare miss sunset if you plan to go!

Oystercatchers, 2900 Bayport Dr., Tampa, FL 33607; (813) 207-6815; oystercatchersrestaurant.com; Seafood/Brunch; $$$$. Spectacular views of the bay, elegant and contemporary decor, highly trained friendly and professional waitstaff, and some of the best seafood Tampa has to offer make Oystercatchers at the Grand Hyatt one of the area's finest restaurants. Seafood is the star of the show at Oystercatchers—the highest-quality fish and ocean-dwelling animals available are artfully prepared in a variety of methods (preferably cooked over the wood-fired grill) and plated beautifully; no detail is overlooked. The meal starts out with the house sourdough bread, which is delightfully sour with a perfect crust and complemented by a high-quality butter and a house oak-smoked sea salt. Next up, an appetizer: go with the amazingly tender calamari fries served with the house signature grilled and caramelized half lemon to squeeze on as a garnish, or the lobster and crab stack with mustard tarragon sauce and brandied horseradish cream. Entrees do a fantastic job of highlighting the natural delicate flavors of the high-quality seafood, more than half of which comes from the Florida and surrounding waters. Fish can be prepared wood grilled, blackened, or sautéed, but true seafood lovers should opt for the wood grill—the lightly smoky char the chefs expertly add to the fish really accents the meat's natural flavors. Coupled with the slightly sweet citrus kick from the charred lemon, it's one of the best seafood plates in all of Tampa Bay. Lunch and dinner at Oystercatchers is a real treat, but it's no secret that their brunch is arguably the best brunch buffet in Tampa. Champagne brunch at Oystercatchers (yes, it comes with unlimited champagne and mimosas) is an absolute feast, featuring a raw bar (with oysters, seared tuna, prawns, and mussels), a pasta station, an omelet station, sushi, caviar, a whole roast, multiple cold salads, over a dozen breakfast-style dishes such as french toast and sausages, an amazing cheese selection (over half a dozen artisan cheeses, each with a complement such as dried fruit, nuts, or honey), and more. Worry not, every sweet tooth in the house will be delighted by the dessert room with chocolate-dipped strawberries, baby crème brûleés, French macarons, a bananas foster station, and more. Any meal at Oystercatchers should be fantastic, but brunch is an experience not to be missed.

Pelagia Trattoria, 4200 Jim Walter Blvd., Tampa, FL 33607; (813) 313-3235; pelagiatrattoria.com; Modern American/Italian; $$$. Sadly, the best-kept secret in Tampa is hiding in plain sight. Well, slightly out of plain sight, which may be the reason thousands of people a day unknowingly walk within a hundred feet of this down-right gorgeous modern Italian-Mediterranean restaurant located at the International Plaza shopping mall. Around the corner and down a flight of stairs from the monotonous chains scattered about Bay Street (the outdoor restaurant row at International Plaza) lies one of the best restaurants in town, Pelagia Trattoria. The interior is a sight to behold, and clearly no expense was spared on the architecture, building materials, or construction of the space with its intricate glass tile work, colorful chandeliers, artful paneling, fantastic backlit vases, flooring, etc. The chefs are strong believers in the Eat Local movement and grow a number of greens, herbs, and veggies right at the restaurant! Upon request (assuming they aren't insanely busy), Chef Andrew Basch is typically more than happy to go outside to the garden and pick something fresh to make a dish for you, and the skilled young man rarely disappoints. The menu is covered with great selections—stone oven pizza makes a wonderful starter, as does the marinated yellow tomato salad with creamy burrata cheese, local basil, and balsamic. The pasta is made in-house and is cooked al dente; it's some of the best pasta anywhere in Tampa. Meat lovers will have a tough time deciding which cut looks the best, but few dishes are visually more impressive than the juicy, perfectly seasoned bone-in rib eye. The filet with *foie gras* truffle butter is also one of the better steaks in town, but that rib eye, oh man. For lighter appetites, small plates fit the bill perfectly and are still powerhouses of flavor—manchego cheese with honeycomb, chorizo with guindilla peppers, and octopus cured with garlic and mint are all fantastic dishes that come in at the $5-to-$6 mark. Whether it be for small plates and a glass of wine (fantastic selection) or one of the best steaks around, Pelagia Trattoria will be a meal not soon forgotten. See Chef Basch's recipes for **BBQ Salmon Salad, Jumbo Lump Crab Cakes, Pomegranate Marinated Duck, Coffee & Cigars,** and **Olive Pâté from Imperia** starting on p. 237.

Specialty Stores, Markets & Producers

Got Tea Teahouse, 2202 W. Waters Ave., Tampa, FL 33604; (813) 930-0470; got-tea.com. Boba tea is a Vietnamese sweet treat, a milk tea served either blended or iced and mixed with milk or cream. What makes boba tea so fun and different from the Western version is the addition of small tapioca "pearls," soft gummy balls about half an inch in diameter and mildly sweet. The tea is mixed and then a plastic layer is placed over the top of the cup and punctured by a straw (just slightly larger in diameter than the tapioca pearls themselves) and when you drink both tea and boba go up the straw for a texture and flavor combination like no other beverage. Got

Tea is a great spot to pop in and try this tasty treat; the small tea shop focuses primarily on boba but also features some quick and easy Vietnamese bites as well. Squid balls, dumplings, and tofu nuggets are some of the bite-size foods Got Tea can whip up upon request, and while they're tasty as can be, the boba tea is by far the can't-miss item on the menu. For whatever reason, they're closed Tues, so visit on any other day and try this fun new Asian drink!

Citrus Park, Westchase, Oldsmar & Town 'N' Country

Citrus Park, Westchase, Oldsmar, and Town 'N' Country are largely bedroom communities, and although the areas are plagued with chain restaurants, there are numerous foodie finds to be had if one knows where to look. This area is primarily west of the Veteran's Expressway, a common artery used for its residents to commute to and from Tampa.

Andy's on the Bay, 472 Douglas Rd., Oldsmar, FL 34677; (813) 855-8166; facebook.com/pages/Andys-On-The-Bay; Cuban; $. Cuban food is soul-warming, hearty, delicious, and filling. Finding good Cuban food often requires traveling to off-the-beaten-path spots, and this particular hole-in-the-wall is no exception. Andy's on the Bay (which isn't technically by any body of water just in case you're wondering) is a little cafeteria that is not visible from any major road but nonetheless is well known among locals and people of Cuban heritage alike. Walk in and you may be underwhelmed; the restaurant doesn't look like much from the outside (or the inside), but order the pork and some black beans and rice and prepare for an explosion of flavor that makes the whole adventure worth it! It's as if you were invited over to someone's Cuban *abuela*'s (grandmother's) home, and she decided to make a special meal for you, roast pork. Andy's also makes a fantastic pork sandwich, with the same roast pork but on Cuban bread, and it's really something special when you add the slightly spicy house "secret sauce," which unlocks a whole new dimension of flavors on what was already a darn solid pork sandwich.

Burger 21, 9664 W. Linebaugh Ave., Tampa, FL 33626; (813) 475-5921; burger21.com; Burgers; $$. Burger 21 was the first entry into the foray of gourmet hamburgers in the Westchase area, and it was quickly followed by drama between the owners and local-celebrity

Chef Chris Ponte (of **Cafe Ponte** in Clearwater [p. 127]). Although Ponte is no longer affiliated with the restaurant, the upscale burger joint still cranks out some tasty 100 percent USDA-Choice burgers! Some burgers not to miss are the Tex-Mex Haystack with smoky Gouda cheese, guacamole, fried onion strings, and chipotle jalapeño sauce on a brioche bun, or the Philly Cheese with grilled peppers and onions, white American and provolone cheeses, and Dijon chive mayo. The fries are equally creative, with selections such as sweet potato fries accompanied by a marshmallow dipping sauce that is an out-of-this-world combination. Hot dogs are also great, as is the chili, but the menu item most necessary to save room for? The Blue Bell ice cream hand-dipped shakes, or the retro floats. Sugar overload, but so worth it.

Catch Twenty-Three, 10103 Montague St., Tampa, FL 33626; (813) 920-0045; catchtwentythree.com; Seafood/Modern American; $$$. Located in the heart of Westchase, Catch Twenty-Three is a seafood restaurant with Latin and Caribbean influence in the cuisine. Only a few years old, the restaurant has already developed a substantial core customer base of regulars who continue to return for the fresh and fun cuisine. The menu has a bit of something for everyone, from sushi rolls to flatbread pizzas, to po'boy sandwiches to Caribbean wings and more, and a clean, inviting space in which to enjoy it. Fridays are known for live Caribbean music and Catch Twenty-Three's great happy hour, which is one of the best known in the neighborhood. A fun, family-friendly spot with good grub, Catch Twenty-Three is a safe bet for a good meal.

El Mofongazo Restaurant, 5522 Hanley Rd., Tampa, FL 33634; (813) 280-2929; elmofongazotampa.com; Puerto Rican; $$. *Mofongo* is as fun to eat as it is to say. A Puerto Rican dish made with fried green plantains that are smashed in a *pilón* (essentially a wooden mortar and pestle) with garlic, olive oil, pork cracklings, and/or bacon. If that didn't already sound tasty enough, it's also available stuffed with seafood and accompanied by a side of fried pork. El Mofongazo Restaurant in Town 'N' Country does a darn good job cranking out some tasty *mofongo* and other Puerto Rican delicious-ness such as the *El Jibarito*—a sandwich where bread is replaced by plantains that are smashed into a somewhat bread-ish shape and fried, and then stuffed full of everything from palomilla steak (the standard) to *morcilla* (blood pudding sausage, which may sound odd but it's fantastic). Add lettuce, tomato, and the garlic aji sauce, and voila, you've got a new favorite sandwich!

One Family Korean Restaurant, 7030 W. Hillsborough Ave., Tampa, FL 33634; (813) 901-0153; onefamilykoreanrestaurant.com; Korean; $$. From the outside, One Family Korean is not an impres-sive restaurant. As you drive past, it appears to be a Laundromat or something equally non–food related, but after sitting down and perusing the menu, it quickly becomes evident that you're sitting in a very authentic Korean restaurant that makes up for what they lack in location and ambiance with variety and flavor. *Gal bi* (short ribs) are thick and meaty, with a bit of sweet and salty kick from the marinade, and the seafood omelet makes a great appetizer (especially for those who've never tried it, what a cool dish). Like most better Korean restaurants, One Family provides a host of different *banchan* (small side dishes to complement your food) such as kimchee, pickled root, sesame bean sprouts, and a really addictive favorite called *ojingeochae muchim*, which consists of dried squid strips reconstituted with spicy fermented soy paste and sesame oil. Few cuisines can match (in a single meal) the depth and breadth of flavors in Korean food, and great Korean food makes for a very memorable meal. At an average cost of around $20 per person, One Family Korean is a bargain for some delicious food!

Pho Quyen, 8404 W. Hillsborough Ave., Tampa, FL 33615; (813) 885-9424; phoquyen.com; Vietnamese; $$. Are you looking for a variety of delicious, authentic Vietnamese dishes but don't want to spend a lot of money? Pho Quyen fits that bill nicely. A family of four could eat at Pho Quyen for less than $10 each if they order tactfully, and dishes like "make your own rolls" or "rice vermicelli" make getting a great value for your money easy. Did "make your own rolls" get your attention? A very engaging dish; after ordering, the waitstaff brings the diner three or four plates: one to assemble the rolls on, one with steamed rice paper (wrappers) stacked on it, one with all the veggies, protein, noodles, peanuts, jalapeños, etc., and a bowl of fish sauce to mix with sriracha (hot sauce) and dunk the rolls in. At a bit less than $9, this is a bargain and more than enough food for one person. Order as an appetizer and the whole table gets to make their food to their own specifications, typically making a huge mess and laughing all the way through. With "Pho" in the name, one would assume the restaurant's pho would be one of its strengths, and it is. PQ's pho is hearty, beefy, and rich with balanced but prevalent spices and seasonings. The traditional pho is recommended, a huge bowl of noodles, veggies, and umami-rich broth with sliced beef, tripe, tendon, flank, and beef meatballs, a steal at $7.

Pipo's Cuban Cafe, 7233 W. Hillsborough Ave., Tampa, FL 33634; (813) 882-0184; pipos.com; Cuban; $$. Cuban food can be found all around Tampa and is typically an excellent value. Pipo's Cuban Cafe is no exception to this rule, and just thinking about their *boliche* (chorizo-stuffed eye round of beef in a savory beef reduction) is enough to make most people begin salivating. If you factor in the price (around $9 with two sides, bread and butter, and iced tea), it's not too painful on the wallet either. Pipo's has a number of specialty sandwiches, such as the ubiquitous Cuban sandwich, or derivatives thereof like the *medianoche* (translates literally as "midnight," a Cuban sandwich on sweet dark egg bread) or the classic guava and cream cheese sandwich called the Big Guava. If you aren't looking for La Segunda Central bakery's fine bread pressed with something inside, there are a number of entrees to choose from. As mentioned earlier, the *boliche* is very satisfying, as is the *picadillo* (ground beef, onions, peppers, olives, capers) and the roast pork (a family recipe that dates back to 1979).

Pizza Fusion, 9556 W. Linebaugh Ave., Tampa, FL 33626; (813) 792-1516; pizzafusion.com; Pizza; $$. The green movement is picking up steam in the Bay area, and one of the restaurants to embrace it the most wholeheartedly is Pizza Fusion. PF is so involved in the sustainable, environmentally friendly, organic, and local food movements that it would take the better part of a page just to list all their valiant efforts to "save the earth, one pizza at a time." All this is very honorable, but it doesn't matter if the pizza isn't tasty! Good news there: on top of being fresh, local, and organic, the pizza is also very flavorful. If someone in your group has a gluten allergy or has an aversion to meat, an extensive number of gluten-free and vegan options are readily available. The menu has a plethora of toppings, and appetizers range from pesto-covered flatbread to meatball sliders. The salads here impress with selections such as the roasted beet and feta with candied walnuts on arugula, or the pear salad with romaine and Gorgonzola cheese. Drinks are a strong suit for Pizza Fusion—they serve a number of artisan teas and sodas and typically have local craft beers on draft at a very reasonable price.

RICE, 7525 W. Hillsborough Ave., Tampa, FL 33615; (813) 889-7766; ricetampa.com; Korean; $$. Korean people love karaoke.

This is immediately evident when walking into RICE restaurant on Hillsborough Avenue and looking to the front of the restaurant: It's a huge stage set up for singing karaoke, which can turn this otherwise quiet restaurant in a strip mall into a really jumping party! If singing (or listening to other people who can't sing take a stab at it) isn't your thing, not to worry. RICE only does karaoke certain nights, and typically later in the night too (once everyone has had a few adult beverages), so there are plenty of quiet opportunities to enjoy the restaurant. Dishes at RICE are very authentic and, as with authentic Korean cuisine, are accompanied by a number of small dishes called *banchan*. *Banchan* are one of the most unique parts of Korean food; it's said that the number of *banchan* that you are served at a meal reflects the caliber of the restaurant you're at, or how important a guest you are if you're at someone's home. The greater the quantity and variety of *banchan*, the more likely it is you're a VIP! If you're new to Korean food, a great staple dish to try on your first visit time is *bi bim bap*, which is a stone hot pot with rice, vegetables, and a fried egg on top, which upon being served (it's a pretty presentation) the diner mixes with hot sauce and scrambles into a more uniform unidentifiable bowl of delicious ricey goodness. Another great dish to try for first-timers and veterans alike is the Korean barbecue, such as *bul go gi* (beef) or *gal bi* (ribs). The sweet, salty, charred barbecue will win a place in any meat lover's heart and will likely have him or her coming back for more. RICE does a number of great authentic Korean dishes and does them well. They even offer sushi, should someone in the group be in the mood for trusty ol' sushi. The dynamic nature of Korean food coupled with the unique manner in which it's presented and consumed makes the meal much more interactive and memorable.

Siam Thai, 9546 W. Linebaugh Ave., Tampa, FL 33626; (813) 475-6999; siamtampa.com; Thai; $$. Westchase isn't blessed with the extensive selection of restaurants that South Tampa is, but there are still some very dependable go-to spots for tasty grub, one of them being Siam Thai. Expectedly, Thai decor fills the room with brightly colored tablecloths protected by glass, paintings, sculptures, golden statues, idols, and more. Pumpkin curry ($13) is one of their better dishes and may be a good selection as it is not available at all Thai restaurants. Pad thai (about $11) and curries (about $11) are also good selections, and they usually please.

Surf Shack Coastal Kitchen, 12217 W. Linebaugh Ave., Tampa, FL 33626; (813) 475-5916; surfshackkitchen.com; Seafood/Tacos; $$. Westchase's go-to spot for Pacific Coast–style tacos is Surf Shack. Locals love the mix of fresh flavors with a bit more crunch from ingredients like cabbage and pickled veggies, along with the additional spice. Creamier ingredients (the chipotle ranch is darn tasty), occasional fruit, and flour tortillas make the food seem much less "heavy." Wraps, burritos, and bowls are also available, but the restaurant's strong suit is said to be its tacos, so that may be the safest place to work with on the menu.

St. Petersburg, Pinellas Park, Largo & Pinellas Beaches

(Pinellas County South of Hwy. 60)

Pinellas County is a quirky area in general. The median age is nearly 20 years older than the median age in neighboring Tampa, which lends to youthful areas developing more modern food into the scene, while retirement communities see more classic eateries thrive. Downtown St. Petersburg has one of the densest concentrations of good restaurants and is a fun area to walk around and explore, while the nearby beach communities make great spots to visit and relax and enjoy the sunset with your toes in the sand.

ABC Seafood, 2705 Fifty-fourth Ave. N., St. Petersburg, FL 33714; (727) 522-1888; Chinese; $$. The name of this restaurant may be quite misleading for most Americans (especially us Floridians), as seeing the word "seafood" in a restaurant title usually evokes images of goofily dressed servers, pieces of boats and mounted fish on the walls, nautical maps, life preservers, etc. ABC Seafood is certainly not that. One of the few authentic Chinese restaurants in St. Petersburg, ABC does have numerous tanks filled with sea-life available for the freshest "catch" possible, but chances of finding hush puppies on the menu are slim to none. Rather modestly decorated (as most authentic Chinese spots typically are), the inside isn't much to speak of in terms of feng shui, although the tanks are fun-looking. People don't really go to ABC for a romantic candlelit dinner; they go for some of the best Chinese in town. The menu is extensive and has multiple excellent dishes. The best plan of attack is to bring as many friends as possible and eat family style (most dishes are served family style anyway, so it's quite conducive to this method of dining), and try everything possible! True Chinese cuisine has some of the most interesting and dynamic mixtures of flavors and textures of any cuisine in the world, and it's available at a comparatively low price, too. Try the salt-and-pepper calamari or the walnut shrimp, or get adventurous and order some tripe or some jellyfish. You may be happy you did!

Alesia, 7204 Central Ave., St. Petersburg, FL 33707; (727) 345-9701; alesiarestaurant.com; Chinese/Vietnamese/French; $$. Blending French, Chinese, and Vietnamese cuisines together yields a really fantastic menu at Alesia in St. Petersburg, where diners can choose from classic, elegant French plates, vibrant, dynamic Asian dishes, or a mixture of both. Menu items are priced to please, with dinner entrees topping out around $17, although most selections are priced under $10, and nearly everything on the menu has a recommended wine pairing printed next to it. Start your meal off with a fantastic bowl of French onion soup, with bacon, baguette, crouton, and gruyère cheese, and some shrimp chips (shrimp-flavored rice chips) with house-made dipping salsa. From there, dive into some pho noodle soup or a *banh mi* sandwich, the latter of which is a beautiful example of French-influenced Asian cuisine (a baguette with pork four ways, pickled veggies, herbs, and jalapeños). Other excellent main course options include delightfully salty, sweet, and rich Chinese short ribs served with potato gratin, or the honey-glazed Cornish game hen, both of which taste as great as they look. The space at Alesia is clean and somewhat minimalist-contemporary although very tastefully done; white walls surround wooden tables and chairs that sit atop concrete floors, creating an inviting dining area. The patio is a fantastic place to dine on a temperate day or a nice evening and is also thoughtfully decorated with similarly simple, clean, inviting decor. Alesia's beer list is one of the best in the area, focusing primarily on higher-quality micro-brews and European selections, both draft and bottle. The wine list is equally impressive and complements the food wonderfully, managing to do so without breaking the bank (selections primarily are priced in the $25-to-$35 range).

Beverly's La Croisette, 7401 Gulf Blvd., St. Pete Beach, FL 33706; (727) 360-2253; beverlyslacroisette.com; French/American/ Breakfast; $. A breakfast favorite for locals and visitors alike, St. Pete Beach staple Beverly's La Croisette cranks out over 3,000 breakfasts per week and boasts that it has more regulars than the nearby bars during happy hour. Rightfully so, as Bev's breakfast is a tasty one, and given that the menu items all have single-digit pricing, it's also quite a popular one, so show up early on weekends, or be prepared to wait! When trying to visualize the menu, think two parts diner and one part French restaurant, and that should get you pretty close. Croissants appear frequently, crepes are readily available, and tasty elevated omelets are a cut above those that you'll find at your typical neighborhood greasy spoon. Beverly apparently has a great sense of humor, too; most of the menu items have clever names and also sound correspondingly delicious, such as the Hangover Omelet (filled with corned beef hash and cheese, topped with hollandaise) or the Campagnard Omelet (filled with diced salami, sautéed onions, covered with swiss, and baked to golden brown). Lunch at La Croisette is just as creative and tasty as breakfast. Sandwiches like the Monte Carlo (filet mignon topped with brie served on a toasted English muffin with Dijon and mayo) are worth the visit alone, and the half-pound burgers are juicy and filling and so customizable even the pickiest diners can get exactly what they want. When visiting St. Pete Beach, a stop at Beverly's La Croisette for breakfast is highly recommended.

Cafe Alma, 260 1st Ave. S., St. Petersburg, FL 33701; (727) 502-5002; cafealma.com; Mediterranean/Seafood/Tapas; $$$. Walking down a flight of stairs into a dark, sexy room is a fitting entrance for one of downtown St. Petersburg's premier tapas restaurants. Exposed brick walls and draping fabrics coupled with soft and pleasant lighting make for a killer ambiance. This spot isn't just good-looking—it can cook, too! An extensive selection of tapas are the menu's focus, with seafood being the protein of choice with a variety of different preparations and ingredients. Pulled duck tacos, herbed goat cheese and crusty bread, and garlic littleneck clams are great ways to start a meal, and you can share dishes like their house specialty paella (with chicken thighs, chorizo, mussels, clams, shrimp, artichokes, and more) or the daily specials for risotto and ravioli, which change with the available fresh ingredients on that day. While Cafe Alma is a popular evening spot for drinks and great food, brunch may be the perfect time to go: The chefs pair tapas and brunch dishes for an impressive menu that really complements their build-your-own Bloody Mary bar. Peppercorn sirloin benedicts, chorizo omelets, towers of french toast—it's all available at Alma. A good-looking restaurant with good-looking staff, good-looking patrons, and a great-looking menu, Cafe Alma is an excellent selection for a meal in St. Petersburg.

Cafe Bohemia, 937 Central Ave., St. Petersburg, FL 33705; (727) 895-4495; thecafebohemia.com; Coffee/Sandwiches/Breakfast; $. Bohemian is a perfect descriptor for this eclectic cafe, where gourmet coffee and tea, pastries, salads, soups, sandwiches, and even craft beers are the stars of the show. Much of the menu is vegetarian and vegan friendly, and menu items mostly have a lot of nutritional value to boot (with the exception of the desserts and sweets, of course). Fittingly eclectic local art covers the walls and is available for sale, while seating options include one of the cushiony couches and half a dozen cafe-style tables. If you're in the mood for a hot sandwich, try the Navigator (wild Alaskan salmon, fresh spinach, tomato, avocado, and goat cheese on mountain bread), or give one of the whole-wheat wraps a shot: The Guru is quite yummy with house-made curried tofu salad, cashews, green apples, cranberries, fresh spinach, and sprouts. Bohemia makes a great cup of coffee, offers numerous specialty drinks, and has high-quality teas brewed to order, available hot or iced. The clientele is typically young and friendly (much like the staff), and the environment is relaxed and inviting. Ample outdoor seating in the adjacent patio is perfect for a nice day; the space is laden with greenery and additional interesting art. Cafe Bohemia is a great spot for anyone on a budget, as the menu tops out at a mere $8, and given the comfortable seating and atmosphere, it's also a fantastic place to relax and read a book with a coffee drink and a healthy lunch.

Cafe Ponte, 13505 Icot Blvd., Clearwater, FL 33760; (727) 538-5768; cafeponte.com; French/American/Asian; $$$$. Few if any chefs in Clearwater are more highly lauded than Christopher Ponte. A Johnson & Wales and Cordon Bleu alum, Ponte has received numerous nods as one of the best chefs in the Bay area. His upscale, elegantly decorated dining establishment just off Ulmerton Road located only minutes away from the St. Petersburg-Clearwater airport is one of the most popular eateries in the area. A meal at Ponte may start with a rich, earthy cup of black trumpet mushroom soup topped with truffled cream, or perhaps the ultra-luxe *foie gras*, every unctuous bite a decadent morsel of seared goodness accented by the sweetness of the poached pear and the lightly tangy amarena cherry reduction. The luxury doesn't end at the appetizer menu. Entrees like corn agnolotti are highlighted with fresh summer truffles, while nine-spice Margaret duck breast gets its own portion of that fantastic *foie gras*, served on a ginger sweet potato pancake with candied kumquat. Seafood lovers will dig happily into the seared salmon with beech mushroom confit and lemon foam, or the miso chilean sea bass, practically dripping with umami and brought to another level with exotic accompaniments like shimeji mushrooms, tamarind-date jam, purple potato puree, and red curry lobster nage. Cafe Ponte's menu is unlike any other in the area and priced accordingly, although not unreasonably. Most appetizers are around $10 and most entrees around $30. An insider tip: A meal can easily be made of multiple appetizers, which also allows diners to better experience what the kitchen is capable of (all at a lower price point and an evening less likely to leave you feeling stuffed).

Cafe Vienna, 5625 4th St. N., St. Petersburg, FL 33703; (727) 527-6404; caffevienna.com; Austrian/German; $$. Old World Austrian and German cuisine, European comfort food served in healthy portions, is the specialty at Cafe Vienna. Pinellas County doesn't have too many spots where you can wash down a nice sauerbraten with a refreshing pilsner, but Cafe Vienna most certainly can satisfy your "wurst" urges for the best Jagerschnitzel around. The interior isn't much to speak of—green walls, red tablecloths, terra-cotta tile floors, and a wooden bar decorated with personalized beer mugs for all the regular schnitzel-addicts—but the inviting warmth of the food more than makes up for the simple decor. Meat is primarily pork and veal, but chicken, fish, and steaks are also available. Although they are perfectly tasty, it seems like a waste to go to a restaurant that does classic German and Austrian dishes so well and order something so Americanized. The flavors in this style of cuisine tend to be more hearty and rich, while not very spicy or bold, so if you're looking for an adventure for your palate, try some of their sauces (the spicy red pepper sauce is good), vinegars, or mustards, and see which pairs best with the different German beers!

Cajun Cafe on the Bayou, 8101 Park Blvd., Pinellas Park, FL 33781; (727) 546-6732; cajuncafeonthebayou.com; Cajun; $$. Sitting on the porch of Cajun Cafe on the Bayou looking out at the water and munching on boudin balls is the closest diners in Tampa Bay can get to actually being in Louisiana without the pesky two-hour flight. Meeting Owner Paul Unwin is half the fun of the experience: You'd expect him to be a laid-back guy with a heavy Creole/Cajun drawl, but he's actually a very enthusiastic Brit with a penchant for food, craft beer, and soccer. Unwin purchased the restaurant from his wife's father (Joe Thibodaux of Thibodaux, Louisiana) in 2003 and took a restaurant that was already good and made it even better. The feel at Cajun Cafe is super relaxed; they even ask that you turn your cell phone off so as not to interrupt your experience, and few if any spots in the area have the unique and relaxing view of the "bayou" that runs along the western perimeter of the restaurant. Food is exactly what you'd expect and hope for: spicy, peppery, well-seasoned Cajun and Creole goodies like crawfish étouffée, fried gator tail, shrimp and oyster po'boys, and numerous different Cajun sausages. Especially addictive and not to be missed are the crawfish corn bread (with crawfish tails baked right in) and boudin balls (a fried peppery sausage and rice ball that is so packed with flavor eating only one may very well prove impossible). Dessert is simple but effective—the Cajun Cafe serves up what is likely the best whiskey bread pudding in all of Tampa Bay (topped with vanilla cream right before serving, it is close-your-eyes good). What better to wash down deliciously spicy and peppery Cajun food than a nice cold microbrewed beer? Unwin keeps a cache of beer on draft and in bottles that will satisfy everyone from beginners to advanced beer lovers, with a fantastic variety of different styles to boot. Cajun Cafe is known for throwing some of the most memorable festivals in the area. People drive for hours and hours to attend the annual crawfish festivals, beer fests, wine events, and other fun celebrations of great food, great music, and great libations. Check their calendar online to catch one of these fun gatherings, and remember, *laissez les bon temps rouler*!

Cassis American Brasserie, 170 Beach Dr. NE., St. Petersburg, FL 33701; (727) 827-2927; cassisab.com; French/American; $$$. Walking through the front door is like teleporting to Europe. No joke. Well, with the exception that the view through the windows of the beautiful trees in Straub Park and sailboats beyond them (it's right on downtown St. Petersburg's Beach Drive) is not what you'd typically see in Paris. Cassis has done a fantastically sexy job replicating a French brasserie, from the white, black, and gray patterned floor tiles (that create a very odd visual illusion of depth) to the exposed yellow accent lighting on the yellow accent walls, or the straight-out-of-France beer tower and tap handles, maybe even the absinthe drip system, complete with spoon. It practically bleeds (yellow of course) European flair. The menu is exactly what you'd expect and exactly what you'd hope for: classic French onion soup (notably well executed), house-made pâté, baked brie, mussels, croque monsieur sandwiches, tartare, and plenty of Old World wine. Larger plates are nothing if not satisfying: duck confit cassoulet with bacon and andouille sausage is hearty, rich, spicy, and large enough to share (although you may choose not to after a bite or two), and braised veal osso bucco with mashed potatoes, bacon, and truffle should be hearty enough to please even the hungriest of diners. Add "fantastic outdoor seating" to the list of accolades, as Cassis' sidewalk tables are covered with big umbrellas to keep customers comfortably shaded while providing an excellent vantage point for some of the finest people-watching in St. Petersburg. *Merci beaucoup*, Cassis!

Jade Bistro, 6139 Park Blvd., Pinellas Park, FL 33781; (727) 544-6186; jade-bistro.com; Vietnamese/Asian; $$. In a nondescript strip mall on the north side of Park Boulevard in Pinellas Park is a Vietnamese restaurant that's a bit of a hidden gem. Interior decor is simple but clean and pleasant: white table linens, soft red high-backed booths along the back wall across from a small bar, and a half dozen tables in the front seating between 4 and 8 each. The menu, however, is a bit more exciting and dynamic. How does spicy oysters prepared tableside with chili sauce, onion, butter, and garlic sound? Does rotisserie quail with lime, salt, and pepper or Vietnamese crepes tickle your fancy?

Those are just starters; the menu gets even more interesting as you continue to turn the pages. Soup lovers can try dishes like oxtail pho noodle soup, or shrimp flake tomato soup with snails, crabmeat, fried tofu, cilantro, chives, and rice noodles, both of which have a depth of flavor well worth the ticket price of $7 to $8. Entrees are equally dynamic—try the signature shaking lamb (cubed lamb marinated with scallions, ginger, rice vinegar, and special sauce) or bring a friend and share the "seven stars around the moon" with fried bacon-wrapped jumbo shrimp, lobster, chicken, and veggies, enough food to feed at least two people and the most expensive menu item at a whopping $22. Jade Bistro is an inexpensive way to try excellent Vietnamese food in a comfortable and clean setting, with a menu worthy of exploration across multiple visits.

Leafy Greens Cafe, 1431 Central Ave., St. Petersburg, FL 33705; (727) 289-7087; leafygreenscafe.com; Vegan/Organic; $$. Herbivores rejoice, there is a restaurant in Downtown St. Petersburg that has tailored its menu such that no animals were harmed in the making of any of the tasty dishes. Given the small footprint of the restaurant, seating is a bit limited with five tables inside and three outside, but that doesn't seem to bother anyone interested in

consuming the organic and meatless grub offered up by Leafy Greens's talented chefs. Pricing is reasonable given the quality and cost of the raw ingredients (and many are truthfully raw), with menu items topping out around $15 and averaging close to $12. Don't discount this spot based on the fact they serve no meat because the menu is flavorful and creatively re-creates healthy organic versions of burgers, tacos, spaghetti, pizza, and more, and goes to show meat isn't necessary to have a good meal. Thought was put into each portion of the menu. Even water is filtered and served with a slice of organic fruit, and high-quality teas are steeped to order. Most everything on the menu is worth trying, but some favorites are the Thai curry soup (with young coconut, avocado, bell pepper, ginger, lime, and zucchini added for flavor and texture) or the from-scratch veggie burger (made with portobello mushrooms, walnuts, sunflower seeds, garnished with raw ketchup and chipotle sauces, and served on romaine leaves in place of a bun). Eating at Leafy Greens is a no-brainer for anyone who doesn't want to compromise flavor when eating healthy, and it's a perfect choice for people with dietary restrictions. Guilt-free and satisfying, Leafy Greens is easily one of the best vegetarian-friendly restaurants in all of Tampa Bay.

Middle Grounds Grill, 10925 Gulf Blvd., Treasure Island, FL 33706; (727) 360-4253; middlegroundsgrill.com; Modern American/Seafood/Steakhouse; $$$$. One of the classier joints in Treasure Island, Middle Grounds Grill does some serious seafood and does it well. Well, in fairness they do most of their dishes quite well, including land dwellers like the espresso-rubbed rack of lamb, the creole egg rolls, or the orange-glazed duck, but seafood is usually the most logical thing to order at a seafood establishment, so seafood is where we'll concentrate. The mango-nut-crusted grouper is pretty much the house favorite dish (grouper crusted in pistachios, walnuts, and macadamias served with a mango beurre blanc sauce over coconut basmati rice; the fish is a fantastic combination of sweet, nutty, and rich and is quite difficult to not order). Coconut almond-crusted shrimp come with a flaky and crunchy crust but remain moist and plump, and are accompanied by a slightly spicy mango habañero dipping sauce. Salads are a strong suit for Middle Grounds—the strawberry shrimp salad with blackened shrimp, feta cheese, and house vanilla bean vinaigrette is a great mix of sweet, salty, and soft, while the orchard salad with duck (spinach, arugula, endive, radicchio, and fennel tossed with bleu cheese, apples, pears, spicy walnuts, and a cider dressing) is crunchy, crispy, earthy, bright, and bitter all at the same time. Someone spent some money decorating the interior of the restaurant, too—booths, lighting, tile work, a large fish tank, wall finishes—everything is clean, attractive, and of good quality. Seafood lovers in the Tampa Bay area laud Middle Grounds as one of the best selections for seafood, and they've maintained a great track record since reinventing themselves half a decade ago (the space spent over 30 years as a pancake house before owners decided to change format).

Mid-Peninsula Seafood, 400 49th St. S., St. Petersburg, FL 33707; (727) 327-8309; midpeninsulaseafood.com; Seafood; $. Simple, fresh, family-owned seafood spots are a Florida staple. Oddly, such restaurants aren't in plentiful supply in the Tampa Bay area, but should you find yourself in St. Petersburg with a hankering for some fresh fried fish, look no further than Mid-Peninsula

Seafood. This place isn't just backing up a Sysco truck out back and unloading pallets of frozen fish fillets from who-knows-where. They're a fish market and a restaurant—they're getting some of the freshest seafood around. Family  owned for over 30 years, Mid-Peninsula has been offering simple yet tasty sea-dwellers prepared grilled, fried, steamed, blackened, or scampi since the 1970s, and it hasn't changed the menu too much since. A rule of thumb with any seafood, the tastiest your meal will be is directly proportional to how recently it left the ocean, so try the fresh catch or daily special, and get it fried; that seems to be what the house does best. They're open lunch and dinner Mon through Sat, but don't try heading in there on Sunday; there'll be a locked door and a sign out front that reads "Gone Fishin"!

The Moon Under Water, 332 Beach Dr. NE., St. Petersburg, FL 33701; (727) 896-6160; themoonunderwater.com; British/Irish/Indian; $$$. While the name may initially sound like a seafood restaurant, The Moon Under Water actually refers to looking up at a coin in a beer, through the bottom of a glass mug. Yep, seriously. That's all you get though; you'll have to Google it to find out the rest (this isn't a history book, you know). The Moon is actually one of the few (probably the only) British-Indian restaurants in St. Petersburg, and it certainly is a popular place. Tables with umbrellas provide shaded outdoor seating while stepping inside the restaurant walls transports you to an upscale British pub where flags hang from the ceiling and classic beer paraphernalia keeps the walls from looking bare. Menu items are a mixture of Indian, British, Mediterranean, and American, with fun plates like the lamb and leek Welsh hot pot with slow-cooked lamb, minted peas, potatoes, and veggies, or the curry-dusted Indian trigger fish with tikha masala sauce, rice, and cardamom. Traditional British pub fare such as bangers and mash or shepherd's pie are also available and well executed. Less adventurous eaters and children also have a good variety of "meat and potatoes" options, and the Moon is known to do a great burger, too.

Munch's Restaurant and Sundries, 3920 6th St. S., St. Petersburg, FL 33705; (727) 896-5972; munchburger.com; Southern; $. Nearly every seemingly simple Southern food (fried chicken, collard greens, corn bread, grits, etc.) is actually an art form that has been passed down from generation to generation, and with the "advent" of fast food, much of that art has been lost to some extent. Fortunately there are restaurant owners and chefs who keep this art alive, and not surprisingly, they quickly develop a fan base of regulars who frequent their establishments for the addictively good food. Munch's fried chicken is so deliciously well executed that it ought to be a controlled substance, and in some regard it is controlled, given that it's a weekly special limited to Tuesday and Saturday. The restaurant does much more than just fried chicken, of course; they have a pretty mean biscuits n' gravy, fried green tomatoes, and a number of other Southern breakfast favorites, all at very reasonable prices. The feel of the restaurant is very much that of a diner, with round swivel stools lined up along a bar and awards, pictures, and paraphernalia strewn about the walls, but people don't eat at Munch's for the aesthetics, they eat there for the darn good Southern food.

Nitally's Thai-Mex Cuisine, 2462 Central Ave., St. Petersburg, FL 33712; (727) 321-8424; nitallys.com; Thai/Mexican; $$. Most people know of Nitally's Thai-Mex Cuisine from their Inferno Soup challenge: Consuming over a quart of the hottest soup imaginable in a half hour (without "losing" any of it) will yield a brave/stupid challenger $1,000 cash and bragging rights throughout Tampa Bay. At the time this was written, no one has ever completed the challenge. The name Nitally's comes from a mixture of the husband-and-wife owners' nicknames: Nit (Kanittha) is from Thailand, and Ally (Allykiro) is from Mexico, which also explains the uncommon fusion of Thai and Mexican cuisines. The menu has popular Thai dishes such as curries, soups, noodles, and stir-fry, and a few Mexican go-to's such as tacos, burritos, and tortilla chips. What sets Nitally's apart are the Thai-Mex creations, including chorizo fried rice (jasmine rice stir-fry with chorizo sausage, garlic, and cilantro), panang mole (red curry, Mexican mole, coconut milk, and sweet basil with chicken, tofu, or shrimp), and chipotle stir-fry with fresh veggies. Any food lover on the hunt for something unique that isn't available anywhere else need look no farther!

The Pearl, 163 107th Ave., Treasure Island, FL 33706; (727) 360-9151; thepearlfinedining.com; Mediterranean/Moroccan/European/American; $$$. Chef Karim Chiadmi is a cool guy. If you ask him (in advance) the man will make you a feast using a goat's head or two, and as odd as that sounds, it's really darn good. The Mediterranean/Moroccan/European/American menu at The Pearl in Treasure Island is a little bit old school and a little bit new school, a little bit adventurous and a little bit textbook. In all likelihood, the more "toned down" and classic dishes are due to the higher median age of the surrounding population, who likely want to eat somewhere nice but don't want to venture outside their comfort zone. Fortunately for diners in the know, getting to nosh on new and exciting plates takes little more effort than buttering up the chef with a compliment or two, and letting him know you appreciate his capability and creativity. The restaurant's interior is painted a very pleasing Moroccan red (that Chef Karim ordered specifically from his homeland), which, coupled with black linens and hanging blue lights, makes for a very inviting dining atmosphere. The wine list is well thought out, with numerous well-known vintners from Napa Valley and surrounding areas, and craft beer is available on draft to boot. One could build a meal simply from the starters menu (and it's not a bad idea given the value and number of selections); baba ghanoush and the tuna martini are great picks, and while more traditional pastas, meats, and seafood are available as main courses, the "Moroccan Specialties" are the way to go (slow braised, fall-apart-tender lamb tagine is cooked in Moroccan spices and herbs and is one of the most aromatic dishes in the house). One of the best restaurants in Treasure Island (if not the best), The Pearl is an adventure for the palate in an inviting setting with a fantastic chef at the helm.

Pia's Trattoria, 3054 Beach Blvd. S., Gulfport, FL 33707; (727) 327-2190; piastrattoria.com; Southern Italian; $$. If you're near Gulfport and in the mood for Italian, go to Pia's. Nestled in cozy downtown Gulfport, Pia's offers up some of the best Southern Italian food in the area, and does so without breaking the bank. Simple yet elegant menu items such as fresh mussels in a roasted almond amaretto sauce or the salmon di capri (smoked salmon with horseradish cream cheese spread with lemon pesto on grilled focaccia) are great ways to kick your meal off with a bang, coupled with a nice glass of Italian wine or beer. Moving into something with a bit more weight to it, pasta dishes such as the *arrabiata* (sun-dried tomato, prosciutto, cracked red pepper, Parmesan) and the pesto rosso (pasta with spicy hazelnut red pesto), or crunchy pressed delicious paninis are as filling as they are tasty, and lovingly crafted using high-quality ingredients. Finish your meal with a nice espresso or cafe Americano; Pia's imports Segafrado Italian coffee beans and has some high-end equipment and the necessary barista experience to make a top-notch after-dinner drink. The space is very comfortable, outdoor bistro tables and chairs are shaded by a large oak tree, while inside has a bit of a cafe feel to it with dark wooden tables, a long bar, and earth-toned tiles and walls. A glass of wine, a panini, and an espresso would be a fantastic way to celebrate a nice Florida day.

Queens Head Eurobar, 2501 Central Ave., St. Petersburg, FL 33713; (727) 498-8584; thequeensheadbar.com; British/Irish/European; $$$. What's in a name? Well, in this particular name, it appears you have a few components: Queens, head, euro, and bar. Queens head—yep, Queen Elizabeth's noggin appears here and there in the decor and especially on the website. There is a huge bar inside that occupies most of the dining room. Queens Head serves seriously flavorful food in a clean and contemporary space that has a whimsical attitude. Outdoor seating is some of the most intriguing in St. Petersburg—white wooden oudoor "beds" with yellow accents are placed in a space where the ground covering is gravel rock, like a funky zen garden from the future. Realistically the beds are just for lounging and enjoying drinks; it is unlikely one could feasibly eat on them. Inside, a large white bar wraps around the kitchen space and has the most seats available for dining of any, while lighting is a mixture of modern lamps and "grandma's chandeliers," and wall space is the same, only this time with antique mirrors and books composing most of the decoration.

Food! The most important part. The food at Queens Head is lightly grounded in British roots but clearly has a lot of bold American flavor influencing the dishes. Start out with the cauliflower cheddar croquettes or the cognac chicken liver pâté—either should get your palate in the mood for the fun to come. The lentil apple salad is an interesting selection: very bright flavors courtesy of poached Granny Smith apples and pickled walnuts, covered in a hibiscus orange reduction. Fish-and-chips, bangers and mash, and shepherd's pie are all available, and all are more flavorful than classic renditions thanks to Chef Scott Jones's clever hand with herbs, spices, and other fresh ingredients, but the roasted pumpkin risotto (with herbed goat cheese and balsamic reduction) and the empire chicken curry (with mint mango chutney and a corn fritter the size of a tennis ball) are where the menu really shines. Desserts are equally fun, gooey sticky toffee pudding is topped with balsamic honey and butterscotch ice cream, while the mocha marshmallow brownie gets a boozy tart kick from some brandied cherries. Dining at Queens Head is a departure from the norm and a considerably enjoyable one.

Red Mesa Cantina, 128 3rd St. S., St. Petersburg, FL 33701; (727) 896-8226; redmesacantina.com; Mexican/Southwestern/Latin American; $$. A favorite of St. Petersburg residents for years, the Red Mesa Cantina (related to, but not to be confused with its sister 4th Street restaurant Red Mesa) brings together Mexican and modern American food into an eclectic fusion of cuisines that should have something for everyone. The restaurant's decor is easily as eclectic as its menu—the main dining area is composed of squared wooden tables with modern-looking white chairs, concrete floors and brick walls, and a very open expo area that peers right into the kitchen. The bar portion of the restaurant has been dubbed the "Lucha Bar" and is decorated with Luchador masks and even metal sculptures of mariachis, and peers out into the patio portion of the restaurant, which serves very nicely for some al fresco dining on more pleasant days. Exactly how eclectic is the menu? Not painfully so, but a number of dishes would likely make a person from Mexico look twice, such as the duck tacos with goat cheese and red chile jelly, or the fried chicken taquitos with chile arbol sauce and *queso fresco*. Other tasty menu items include the ceviches (there are half a dozen to choose from), the sirloin chorizo burger (with Pepper Jack cheese, fried onions, and chipotle aioli), and the duck confit *torta* (a sandwich with arugula, rajas, caramelized onions, and guacamole). This trendy spot gets pretty busy on weekends; reservations aren't required but they sure wouldn't hurt, and remember the Lucha Bar is open seating so first come, first served.

Señor Taco, 6447 Park Blvd. N., Pinellas Park, FL 33781; (727) 289-7080; senortacopinellas.com; Mexican/Tacos; $. Hopefully there is a visible trend in this book with regard to finding the best ethnic restaurants. They are typically small, mom-and-pop shops with minimalist decor, inexpensive dishware and silverware, no aesthetically redeeming qualities, and absolutely delicious food. Señor Taco fits this description quite well. Husband and wife Cesar and Cynthia Sosa came to sunny Florida directly from the Yucatan region of Mexico and brought their delicious native food with them. It doesn't take a Rhodes scholar to figure out what the specialty of the house is (tacos), and shortly after biting into one, it wouldn't take a caveman to figure out exactly why they are. The tacos are nothing like what you'd find at a national fast-food chain taco spot; they are house-made soft corn tortillas with cilantro, onion, and salsa, and meats like *carnitas* (fried pork), chorizo (spicy sausage), and *cochinita pibil* (essentially a citrus-rubbed "Mayan barbecue" pork shoulder, roasted in-house). These tacos are substantially more flavorful and authentic than any you may be served by a Spanglish-speaking Chihuahua. Promise. Señor Taco's menu has other tasty items worth trying such as *tortas* (Mexican sandwiches on fluffy bread filled with the same meat the tacos are) and a host of other larger stuffed items. Try the "Machete" taco, a larger and more filling taco with a blend of meats. Given that tacos are approximately $2 each and taste fantastic, it's no surprise that Cesar sells hundreds a day to happy patrons who drive from all over Pinellas County for some of the best Mexican food around.

Skyway Jack's, 2795 34th St. S., St. Petersburg, FL 33711; (727) 867-1907; Breakfast; $. Skyway Jack's is a fun breakfast/lunch

spot known for its
fantastic pancakes
(said to be the best
in St. Pete) and makes
a great local mom-and-
pop alternative to a "greasy spoon"
chain restaurant. The service alone is worth the visit—the very welcoming servers give the restaurant a feel akin to breakfast at your
grandmother's house, assuming your grandmother was a pancake
ninja. Skyway Jack's can do a lot more than just make pancakes (I
mean, come on, there's an egg in a tuxedo and top hat out front
for crying out loud); try their scrapple (pork and cornmeal goodness
with eggs, taters, and a biscuit, named "Best Breakfast in Florida"
by *Food Network Magazine*) or the scrambled brains (pork brains
scrambled with eggs served like most dishes with taters and a biscuit). Their sense of humor doesn't stop with the cleverly named
menu items—servers wear shirts with a bit of "signature breakfast
innuendo," if you will: two purposefully placed eggs across the
chest with (might as well just say it) yolk nipples. The egg-boobs
branding appears frequently around the restaurant, on everything
from coffee mugs to the pig-server cartoon stickers on the windows,
delightfully unprofessional and strangely inviting. A bargain if ever
there were a bargain, breakfast for two at Skyway Jack's will almost
always run less than $20 and is rarely anything less than satisfying.

St. Pete Brasserie, 539 Central Ave., St. Petersburg, FL
33701; (727) 823-6372; stpetebrasserie.com; French; $$$. Although

adorned in more clean and contemporary rather than classic French brasserie decor, St. Pete Brasserie does offer up some of the better French food in the 'Burg (a common nickname for St. Petersburg). Onion soup, artisan cheeses, pâtés and mousses, carpaccio, escargot, mussels, oysters, and more are available on the Franco-centric menu, while fans of more domestic food will still be able to enjoy steaks, hamburgers, fish, and more. The atmosphere is hip and lively, and given its location on Central Avenue, it is a popular place with the trendy, young professional crowd. Most of the food is on the richer side (it's baffling to many that French people are typically quite thin while their cuisine is among the richest in the world), but the restaurant offers vegetarian and lower-carb options, so don't let the concept that all French food is unhealthy deter you from checking out this tasty brasserie!

Sushi Rock Grill, 1163 Dr. Martin Luther King Junior St. N., St. Petersburg, FL 33701; (727) 898-7625; thesushirockgrill.com; Sushi/Seafood; $$$. One of St. Petersburg's most loved sushi spots, Sushi Rock Grill has been serving up fish and rice to devoted regulars for years. Upon entering the restaurant, diners can't miss the beautiful long cherry-colored wooden sushi bar, with cobalt blue accents overhead and earth-tone tiles and walls throughout the restaurant. The rest of the restaurant is decorated using the same wood and blue accents, and it is very clean and inviting. A good variety of seafood is available for those desiring nigiri and sashimi, including less common goodies like amaebi (sweet shrimp), surf clam, and escolar (white tuna). Sushi Rock's fish is fresh and rolls are fun and approachable, albeit a bit Americanized, commonly using ingredients like cream cheese and mayonnaise, and offerings of entire rolls deep fried. While the menu at SRG may lack authenticity, it certainly doesn't lack flavor. The Mama Son roll wraps chopped scallops and avocado with grilled barbecue eel and is both sweet and rich, while the Crystal Roll offers a crunchy and herby punch of flavors by mixing spicy tuna, pickled daikon, cilantro, cucumber, and wasabi-flavored fish roe, all wrapped up in rice paper. The restaurant also offers ample outdoor seating, with a relaxing Asian garden feel and walls to help keep the sounds of passing traffic muted. If you or your group are hungry for sushi in St. Petersburg, Sushi Rock Grill should fit the bill nicely.

Taste of Punjab, 6540 Park Blvd., Pinellas Park, FL 33781; (727) 545-4103; tasteofpunjabindiancuisine.com; Indian; $$. So often Indian restaurants err on the side of caution when adding heat to dishes for non-Indian diners, but Taste of Punjab fearlessly forges ahead in the war against bland curries, kormas, and vindaloo. Chef-Owner Rajinder Singh offers up an extensive menu of delicacies from his home country, and he executes them with tact and talent to the point that many local food lovers consider his food to be the best Indian available in the area. Decor isn't anything fancy or elaborate; tables and booths from decades past make up the dining area, and were it not for the occasional painting depicting a palace or scene from India, at first glance this restaurant could just as easily serve fried chicken as it could Indian food. The lunch buffet is a daily changing selection of approximately a dozen different dishes, and it's a bargain, coming in just a hair under $9. As great as lunch is, dinner is the time to visit and bringing friends in order to share a number of Punjab's excellent dishes is highly recommended. Taste of Punjab has an impressive selection of fresh baked breads available, from the ever popular clay-oven flatbread naan to less commonly seen breads like *roti* and *chapati* (like naan but thinner),

bhatoora (a big fried hollow puff of bread the size of a football), *kulcha*, *paratha*, and more. The bread isn't the only impressive component of the menu—the spicy vindaloo is one of the restaurant's strongest offerings (choose from goat, lamb, chicken, beef, and seafood), and one of the spiciest to boot. Even sides such as yogurt and *raita* are excellent, as are the various chutneys (mango, mint, tamarind, and onion are available), and the *achaar* pickles are surprisingly addictive. Vegetarians will be happy to discover there are dozens of meat-free options at Punjab, and none is lacking flavor from the absence of meat, so worry not, herbivores!

Verducci's Pizzeria & Trattoria, 937 Central Ave., St. Petersburg, FL 33705; (727) 895-4495; verduccisstpetebeach.com; Pizza; $$. St. Pete Beach residents know where to go to get some darn good made-from-scratch Italian food and some tasty pizza: Verducci's Pizzeria & Trattoria. Large portions and reasonable prices are the status quo at Verducci's, where Owners Vinny Fortunato and Giovanni Scamardella keep the restaurant smelling drool-inducingly good 7 days a week. Many of the regulars claim that the restaurant serves up the best pizza in St. Petersburg, that the lasagna is the melt-in-your-mouth thing dreams are made of, and that it keeps them coming back week after week. Other menu highlights include the caprese salad with a delicious dollop of baby mozzarella cheese, fresh basil, and a balsamic reduction, or the pillowy soft gnocchi, and the hearty chicken Francese, which also keep diners returning regularly. Beer and wine are inexpensive but the selection isn't very exotic, and the restaurant also features drink specials frequently and has TVs and darts, so it wouldn't be a bad place to watch a sports game either. Just the smell inside is worth the visit, but fans of pasta dishes will appreciate the work that went into making much of the menu fresh and from scratch, and can often enjoy watching Owner Vinny lovingly craft what will soon become their meal in the open portion of the kitchen. Calzones are another strength of Verducci's, not surprisingly though given that they are composed of the same ingredients as the pizza pies. Great pizza and food that tastes like your Italian grandmother made it are reason enough to put Verducci's near the top of your list!

Wood Fired Pizza and Wine Bar, 344 1st Ave. S., St. Petersburg, FL 33701; (727) 282-1888; wood-firedpizza.com; Pizza; $$$. Peter Taylor's new outpost in Downtown St. Petersburg, only this time strategically located adjacent to a multi-tap beer bar. See description for original location in North Tampa, p. 74.

Z Grille, 104 2nd St. S., St. Petersburg, FL 33701; (727) 822-9600; zgrille.net; Modern American; $$$. The chic, contemporary interior of Z Grille is one of St. Petersburg's most ultra-modern spots, with a pretty modern American menu to boot. The floor in the dining area is a wooden "wave" that seamlessly transitions from the floor into the wall, and then again into the ceiling for a remarkably unique feeling, almost as though you were dining inside an artistic rendition of a skateboarder's half-pipe. Opposite the "wave" are floor-to-ceiling windows with opaque squares artfully staggered, likely also to help cut down on echoes (which are the only downside to the beautiful decor; the restaurant when busy is anything but quiet). Remaining (non-wood) walls and floors are concrete while tables are stainless steel and chairs a European-looking white. Wine selection is great, and bottles in cleverly constructed racks create an attractive wall covering at the rear of the restaurant. Staff is as attractive as the dining space, and Chef-Owner Zach Gross keeps the menu fun and interesting. Items like the chili-glazed Dr Pepper fried ribs are well seasoned, sweet, and tangy, accompanied by a sesame slaw, while the house-favorite deviled eggs are rich, earthy, and a bit piquant from the mustard. The menu includes a bevy of cleverly named and con-structed dishes, such as the BBBLT (yes, that means Bacon, Bacon, Bacon, Lettuce, and Tomato) or the over-the-top umami-bomb of a *foie gras* steak-burger (with Neuske's bacon, grilled onions, *foie gras*, and truffled fries) should satisfy anyone looking for elegant comfort food and do so without breaking the bank (any meal with truffles, steak, and *foie gras* priced at only $21 is a pretty solid deal). Prices are reasonable, but frequent visitors and locals know that happy hour is where the bargains are to be had. Show up between 4 and 6:30 p.m. and enjoy lower prices on food and half-off bottles of wine!

Landmarks

Bella Brava, 204 Beach Dr. NE., St. Petersburg, FL 33701; (727) 895-5515; bellabrava.com; Italian; $$$. Bella Brava is a contemporary, well-decorated space in a primo location on Beach Drive, Downtown St. Petersburg's place to see and be seen. A modern Italian eatery that serves as a popular destination for the well-dressed and well-heeled crowd, Bella Brava is as much a spot to hang out and have drinks as it is a restaurant. Beef carpaccio is a nice way to start a meal: peppery seared tenderloin is shaved paper thin and accented with shaved parm, fried capers, bitter arugula, and a horseradish cream sauce that hits the palate from so many different angles it's hard not to like. Flatbreads are particularly enjoyable at Bella Brava, and the Fichi & Rucola is an excellent offering (figs, pancetta, Gorgonzola cheese, arugula, and balsamic), while cheese lovers often opt for the *quattro formaggio* flatbread with parm, asiago, fontina, and tallegio (just smelling this one is a treat) and for a bit of additional herbal aromatics, sage is added prior to cooking in the wood-stone oven. Bella Brava offers a variety of pasta dishes and classic entrees, and naturally soups and salads are available too. Outdoor seating is a great spot to do some people watching and enjoy the beautiful views of the neighboring parks and marinas, and BB advertises that they have the longest-running happy hour in the area, so it's not a bad spot to sit and enjoy a cocktail or a glass of wine either!

Ceviche, 10 Beach Dr., St. Petersburg, FL 33701; (727) 209-2299; ceviche.com; Spanish/Tapas; $$$. Live guitarists and flamenco dancers make Ceviche in Downtown St. Petersburg's Ponce de Leon Hotel a nightlife hot spot enjoyed by young and old alike. Large windows surround the dining area and offer a view of passersby, while the downstairs portion of the restaurant is a bar (dubbed "Pincho y Pincho"), which is more suited to a less formal, more convivial atmosphere. The lively feel of Ceviche's bar is ideal for enjoying a glass or three of sangria along with some tasty tapas, and there is no shortage of tapas available—choose from over 100! Although the restaurant is a fun place to hang out solo, meals are best shared with friends, as tapas make fantastic communal dishes. Start a meal off with one of the six house ceviches or a few *tapas frias* (cold plates). The *boquerones* (anchovies on crostini with sweet onion and cilantro relish) and the *calamares* (grilled squid with herbs and sweet peppers) are a couple of great selections. Salads are fun and interesting—try the *ensalada de pato* (baby greens with walnuts, fennel, pears, and figs, topped with smoked duck) for a great flavor punch. When progressing to the *tapas calientes* (hot plates) portion of the menu, give the meaty *piquillos rellenos* (roasted red peppers stuffed with veal and chorizo) a try, or the earthy and rich *caracoles a la vasca* (escargot with a sherry cream sauce in puff pastry). Truthfully one could visit Ceviche a dozen times and still never try the entire menu, although it would be a delicious challenge to undertake!

Chattaway, 358 22nd Ave. S., St. Petersburg, FL 33705; (727) 823-1594; thechattaway.com; Seafood/Burgers; $$. There is a restaurant in St. Petersburg that has been serving hamburgers since the 1940s and has been open since the Prohibition era, known as the Chattaway. Originating as a grocery store in 1922, the Chattaway evolved and changed hands multiple times but never lost its soul or its welcoming feel. The menu is nothing elaborate—hamburgers and sandwiches, soups, salads, and fried sides. But Chattaway offers a unique environment with more history than most other restaurants in the area and its own flavor of Florida. The dining room is decorated with old plates and pictures, a ceiling painted to mimic the cloudy sky, and a hodgepodge of tables and chairs that look to have been sourced from a dozen different garage sales. Outdoor seating has equal amounts of character: Large potted plants enclose a courtyard with tables scattered about and a long covered "Chattabar" where diners can enjoy a frosty beer or three with their burger. Dining at the Chattaway is more of an entertaining experience than it is a foodie adventure, although the house signature Chattaburger is 7 ounces of ground beef tasty enough to win a local newspaper award for being the "Best Hamburger in Tampa Bay" in 2010.

Guppy's, 1701 Gulf Blvd., Indian Rocks Beach, FL 33785; (727) 593-2032; 3bestchefs.com; Seafood; $$$. Indian Rocks Beach's favorite seafood restaurant is Guppy's, and it's no secret. Locals and tourists alike fill the booths at Guppy's on a regular basis, and in the busy season, make a reservation because the place stays packed pretty continuously. Given the name Guppy's, one could easily guess that seafood is naturally the specialty here, and the restaurant caters to both young and old (the senior crowd is fond of the dinner times that start at 4 p.m.), families, couples, and singles. Decor is what one would expect in a good-quality Florida seafood restaurant: tile floors, earth-toned walls, nice wooden tables inside with great patio seating outside, an inviting bar, and cozy booths should you want to get away from the noise. Guppy's menu isn't pushing any culinary envelopes; its menu is very approachable to eaters of all comfort levels and should be able to provide something for everyone, regardless of the occasion or the mood.

Marchand's, 501 5th Ave. NE., St. Petersburg, FL 33701; (727) 894-1000; marchandsbarandgrill.com; Modern American; $$$$. Marchand's is a beautiful restaurant in a beautiful hotel in a beautiful part of waterfront Downtown St. Petersburg. Sounds beautiful, right? Everything about a restaurant can be attractive, but if the food falls short, it's simply a pretty space with "blah" food. Not the case for Marchand's: the food is as enjoyable as the aesthetics—high ceilings, beautiful wood and tile floors, modern art, and a fantastic bar that acts as a centerpiece for the dining space. Menu items are primarily classics with a twist, along with a handful of dishes unique to the restaurant itself, such as the particularly satisfying mix of sweet, smoky, and nutty "Grilled Peaches & Plums" with candied pistachio and warm bacon dressing. Marchand's offers an impressive number of menus. In addition to the breakfast, lunch, and dinner menus, there is a sushi menu (with a dozen or two options for rolls and sashimi), an afternoon tea menu (with homemade tea sandwiches and pastries, naturally), a "classic" 1925 menu (a prix-fixe three-course for $19.25), and a Blue Ribbon menu, bringing half a dozen favorites from Manhattan's Blue Ribbon restaurants into Florida. While all this seems like a vast array of dining options for one restaurant, the most celebrated meal at Marchand's has not yet been mentioned: brunch. Champagne brunch, to be more exact, and with more gourmet stations (seafood, pasta, omelet, sweets, etc.) than you can shake a breadstick at, Marchand's Sunday midday meal is heralded as one of the best in the Bay.

Maritana Grille, Loews Don CeSar Hotel, 3400 Gulf Blvd., St. Pete Beach, FL 33706; (727) 360-1882; loewshotels.com/en/restaurants/the-maritana-grille; Seafood; $$$$. **Inside St. Pete Beach's** historic waterfront Don CeSar hotel is a very classy restaurant that goes by the moniker "Maritana." Classic fine-dining decor of neutral-colored walls, white tablecloths, and expensive fixtures is offset by beautiful blue accents (dishware, fish tanks, etc.) in this high-end seafood establishment. Well-behaved and well-dressed servers provide traditional high-end service and very expediently bring out high-quality seafood (and earth dwellers too, for people not in the mood for creatures that swim) in rich sauces and with decadent sides. Menu items also have an element of creativity and fun to them: duck confit wontons take an inexpensive Asian appetizer and put an elegant spin on it, while diver scallop carpaccio with wasabi-tobiko aioli celebrates seafood in its most naked form, unheated. While entree features of land animals and fowl are well constructed (braised rabbit with mushroom risotto or coffee-rubbed NY strip with onion-potato bread pudding are both yummy selections when available), seafood is king at Maritana, available prepared sous vide, cast-iron griddled, or more traditionally grilled and blackened; expect a top-notch fish on your dish, as you wish. Given the prices at Maritana, one would expect no less than excellent food and service, as dinner for two with drinks frequently exceeds $150.

Mazzaro's, 2909 22nd Ave. N., St. Petersburg, FL 33713; (727) 321-2400; mazzarosmarket.com; Italian; $$. Mazzaro's is an Italian market. Mazzaro's is THE Italian market. Mazzaro's is one of, if not the most impressive Italian markets in the state of Florida. Mazzaro's is a butcher, a deli, a coffee shop, a wine and craft beer store, a cheese shop, a pasta maker, a bread baker, a popular lunch destination, and a source for hundreds of artisan imported food items. Mazzaro's most trafficked and popular day by far is Saturday, when people drive from all over the Bay area to pick up delicious homemade quality goods, foods, cheese, wine, and more, and it can be a bit of a madhouse. Scratch that actually, it is pretty consistently the busiest market/restaurant anywhere near its location (which is in a bit of an oddball spot on 22nd Avenue North in St. Petersburg). Looking for baked goods? Mazzaro's makes more than half a dozen different kinds of bread, cookies, cakes, and pastries, and some fantastic biscotti. Want a cold and sweet treat? They make gelato fresh daily. Looking for meat and seafood? Experienced butchers will guide you through different cuts and types of high-quality beef, lamb, poultry, and more, while numerous different fish are available, many of which are locally caught. Hooked on the bean? Mazzaro's will roast coffee for you to take home and has baristas on-site to make fantastic coffee beverages for you while you wait. Offering great food and top-quality products, Mazzaro's is a tough spot to beat when trying to track down delicious Italian specialties in the Bay.

Salt Rock Grill, 19325 Gulf Blvd., Indian Shores, FL 33785; (727) 593-7625; saltrockgrill.com; Seafood; $$$$. Indian Shores's benchmark for seafood restaurants also has one of Pinellas County's best views from an eatery, the Salt Rock Grill. Sister restaurant to Clearwater hot spots **Island Way Grill** (p. 171) and **Rumba Island Bar & Grill** (p. 185), Salt Rock has been serving up fresh seafood to vacationers and loyal regulars for years, and it continues to garner attention, awards, and excitement as time goes on. Fresh seafood may be Salt Rock's specialty, but lovers of a good steak will be excited to know that the restaurant uses top-quality cuts of house-aged USDA Prime beef and cooks them at 1200°F over a citrus and oak wood pit fire, lending a great char and smoky flavor to an already tasty piece of meat. Looking out at the Intercoastal while dining is a sight to see, and Salt Rock's dining space is surrounded by windows, windows, and more windows so every diner has a water view to complement their food, which has made them one of the most popular restaurants in the area. Raw bar aficionados are often impressed by SRG's selection of fresh oysters (they offer nearly a dozen varieties), and sushi fans will appreciate the teriyaki-glazed seared tuna with ginger aioli, or the Frankie's Tuna Roll appetizer. Wine lovers are also in for a treat: Hundreds of selections are available from all over the world and at a wide variety of price points, and microbrewed beer is available for those not in the mood for grape juice. Salt Rock covers all the bases, fresh and flavorful food, good service, great wine selection, and a fantastic view. It's no surprise it's considered one of the best restaurants in the area.

Ted Peters Famous Smoked Fish, 1350 Pasadena Ave. S., South Pasadena, FL 33707; (727) 381-7931; Seafood; $$. Ted Peters Famous Smoked Fish has been smoking delicious mullet, salmon, mackerel, and mahimahi for well over 50 years, and it has diners all across the Bay area hooked. When the restaurant was featured on the Food Network's show *Diners, Drive-ins and Dives* Guy Fieri went specifically to Ted Peters to figure out what all the commotion was about, and he had a great experience and enjoyed some great smoked fish while hanging out with the cooks. The restaurant has outdoor and indoor seating, and only takes cash, although there is an ATM at the restaurant if you forget to bring any. The menu is pretty basic; smoked fish and smoked fish spread are what has put the place on the map, and missing out on those would be a shame, but many praise Ted's cheeseburger as one of the best in the area. Drinks, sides, beer, and wine are all inexpensive and in limited selection, which isn't really a concern given that most visitors at TP's are there for one thing—the smoked fish.

Area anglers love Ted's, because for a dollar a pound they can get their fresh catch smoked for them, eliminating the hassle of setting up a smoker and assuring it'll be done correctly over local Florida red oak. Take a trip to St. Petersburg and enjoy this classic piece of Bay area food history. You'll be glad you did.

Dunedin, Palm Harbor, Clearwater, Tarpon Springs & Safety Harbor

(Pinellas County North of Hwy. 60)

Pinellas County north of Highway 60 has numerous little towns, each with its own feel, culture, history, and food scene. Tarpon Springs has the highest per capita concentration of Greek people in the USA, and naturally this is where one would go to find great Greek food, while Dunedin is a great town to walk around and shop in, exploring the various breweries, restaurants, bars, and more.

Besa Grill, 2542 N. McMullen Booth Rd., Clearwater, FL 33761; (727) 400-6900; besagrill.com; Latin American/Modern American; $$$. One of Clearwater's newest hot spots, Besa Grill serves up food with modern flair to match the very sleek and sexy panache of its decor. The restaurant was very welcomed to the chain-laden Countryside area of Clearwater and immediately became a hit with surrounding neighborhoods as the go-to spot with fun food and a lively bar. The fare can best be described as Latin American fusion with a bit of a modern twist. Duck nachos are a great plate to share, with black bean corn salsa and avocado crema, or the Ceviche Scoop, a scoop of the chef's daily creation of ceviche served in an avocado half. Flatbreads are tasty and easy to share, the braised short rib is beefy, rich, sweet, smoky, and spicy, topped with applewood bacon, blue cheese, caramelized onions, and horseradish crema, while the Shrimp + Chorizo has a bit more of a spicy pop from the chorizo, nicely complemented by roasted red peppers, zesty tomato sauce, and chiuaua cheese. Seafood is flown in fresh and is a mixture of rich, spicy, and dynamic like most of the menu. Sea bass, grouper, and salmon are all tasty and presented beautifully. Diners in the mood for something simpler can try one of Besa's fire-grilled steaks, flown in from Stockyards Chicago Angus and aged 28 days for ideal flavor, or perhaps some fish tacos with pico de gallo, napa cabbage, cilantro, and crema. Even the burger at Besa is great, a half pounder, Angus beef, with a portobello mushroom cap, fire-roasted red peppers, swiss cheese, arugula pesto, and a brioche bun, accompanied by some fantastic yucca fries. If you haven't tried yucca fries yet, that's a shame and they need to be put on your bucket list immediately. With the plethora of house-made, unique, and delicious sauces at Besa from the guava barbecue to the Serrano-agave orange marmalade used to coat the pork medallions prior to grilling, and the sexy atmosphere and modern decor, it's no wonder Besa Grill became a huge hit shortly after opening.

The Black Pearl, 315 Main St., Dunedin, FL 34698; (727) 734-3463; theblackpearlrestaurant.com; American/French; $$$$. What it lacks in size, it more than makes up for with food and service. The Black Pearl is Dunedin's high-end fine-dining establishment and carries the torch of fine wine, crystal glassware, and classically trained waitstaff and cookstaff in its cozy ten-table Downtown location. Many restaurants have discarded polish and refinement in favor of comfort and a lively atmosphere, but The Black Pearl believes in true fine dining. A pleasant, knowledgeable, and experienced server will tend to your every need while the same caliber of chefery in the kitchen will see to it that your dish is executed flawlessly. And you will pay for it. Not an unreasonable amount, mind you; the appetizers mostly run in the $10-to-$20 range, and entrees are $35 and under, with a salad, starch, and veggie included. The menu is unapologetically bathed in cream sauces, butter, sherry, brandy, bacon, pâté, and everything else that is right with the world. The Black Pearl is more geared toward special occasions and people who are having a meal to enjoy a meal, not to drive themselves insane counting calories. Butternut squash ravioli is smooth and slightly earthy with a sweet umami layer from its cranberry butter sauce, while escargot en pâté *feuilletee* is every bit as decadent as you want it to be, each tender snail morsel a delight for the senses, swimming in garlic butter cream beneath the puff pastry shell. Oh, and those are just appetizers. Entrees are equally luxe. Veal paillards come coated in a vanilla bean sauce and accompanied by exotic mushrooms, while Long Island duckling is done two ways, braised (if you were thinking about the legs) and grilled (should you be eyeing the breasts). A meal that will almost assuredly impress, dinner at The Black Pearl won't soon be forgotten.

Casa Ludovico, 1710 Alt. 19 N., Palm Harbor, FL 34683; (727) 784-7779; eatatcasa.com; Italian; $$$. Casa Ludovico is unquestionably a "casa": The restaurant is a house that was built over a century ago and was the former home of the president of Southern College (which burned down in a fire in the 1920s and was relocated to Lakeland, Florida). Since then the home has housed owners of a citrus grove and become a daycare center, an antiques shop, and now an Italian restaurant. Naturally, the fact that the restaurant is a house gives it a very homey, comfortable feeling, and the fact that they serve tasty and comforting classic Italian dishes only helps in making dinner a relaxing and enjoyable experience. Antipasti are the perfect beginning to a meal at Ludovico; the *rollatine di melanzane* is a ricotta, basil, and tomato-stuffed rolled eggplant dish that is flavorful without being too heavy, while the *carpaccio di manzo malatesta* takes seared and shaved top-quality beef and accents it with bitter arugula and aged Parmesan. Entree courses are organized primarily by protein—the menu has a handful of options for chicken dishes, fish, steak, veal, and pasta, which naturally has the most variety of selections. Linguine, fettuccini, rigatoni, penne, ravioli—whatever your pasta pleasure, Ludovico has you covered.

Casa Tina, 365 Main St., Dunedin, FL 34698; (727) 734-9226; casatinas.com; Mexican; $$. Dunedin's favorite Mexican restaurant is the popular downtown mom-and-pop spot called Casa Tina. Tina and Javier Avila (ex–Señor Frogs owners who started in Mexico and moved to Miami) created the restaurant in 1991 and have grown and grown from small beginnings to a successful and well-known Downtown favorite, with a few quirky idiosyncrasies—the owners will let you know up front that you may have to yell for a server, and that Rome wasn't built in a day, so neither was your fresh, made-to-order meal, and it might take a few minutes to cook! Casa Tina cooks up a lot of Mexican favorites, including some great authentic dishes that are harder to find in the states. Chances are you've had tacos, burritos, and enchiladas, so let's focus on the more interesting stuff. *Chayote relleno* is a dish that may seem less familiar but is delicious, a buttery-flavored steamed squash filled with onions, bread crumbs, garlic, and toasted almonds, fun and filling for only $5. Mexico has some fantastic soups that don't always make it across the border, so try the *posole* (a spicy chicken stew with hominy and ancho chilies) or the *sopa tarasca* (a pinto bean soup with crema, *cotija* cheese, tortilla strips, and *guajillo* pepper). The specialties of the house are the way to go for entrees; try the slightly spicy and slightly chocolatey (no kidding) mole *poblano* with a rich, sweet, thick mole sauce served with chicken or veggies on an enchilada, or give the *chiles en nogada* a go (a duo of picadillo-stuffed poblano peppers topped with a brandy-walnut cream sauce and pomegranate seeds). From mild to wild, if Mexican food is on the radar, make Casa Tina the target.

Costa's, 521 Athens St., Tarpon Springs, FL 34689; (727) 938-6890; costascuisine.com; Greek; $$. Family-owned hole-in-the-wall Greek restaurants in Tarpon Springs aren't typically known for their exemplary and prompt service, modern decor, or fine dishware (does "OPA!" ring a bell?), but they are known for tasty food and an inexpensive meal, which is the more appealing quality to most food lovers. Costa's is no exception. Decor may not have changed much since the restaurant opened in the 1970s, the dishware is simple, and service can be spotty, but all this is worth it to people on the hunt for authentic Greek food. Charbroiled octopus is the dish most of the foodies rave about at Costa's, available in a number of dishes, but most specifically the Grecian octopus (charred octopus served with feta cheese, garlic, jalapeño, lemon, and olive oil). Yum. *Dolamades* (grape leaves stuffed with ground beef and rice, topped with an egg-lemon sauce) are well-proportioned amounts of beef and rice, well-seasoned, and have a nice rich lemony kick from their sauce topping. Try the Spread Combo, a combo of three of Costa's spreads. *Melitzanosalata* (eggplant), *taramosalata* (Greek caviar), and *tirokafteri* (spicy feta) are three great selections. Costa's has over a dozen great seafood entrees; try the fried hannous, a whole fried sea bass, or the slow-roasted lamb with homemade gravy, if seafood isn't your thing. For a show with dinner, try the *saganaki* (a pan-seared casseri cheese, flambéed tableside and extinguished with lemon juice, served with bread). And don't burn yourself!

Delco's Original Steaks and Hoagies, 1701 Main St., Dunedin, FL 34698; (727) 738-4700; delcosoriginal.com; Cheesesteaks/ Sandwiches; $. We Floridians call them cheesesteaks, but to Philly natives they're just "steaks." This would explain why Delco's Original Steaks and Hoagies doesn't sell steaks, but they do make one of the best cheesesteaks in the Bay area. Pennsylvania natives will be happy to know Delco's ships in their bread from Amoroso's bakery (arguably the most crucial component); the rib eye, the peppers, the cheese, essentially every component of the sandwich comes from the sandwich's hometown, as does most of the lunch meat, the Herr's potato chips, and the Hank's sodas. Diners in the mood for a steak who don't want to eat beef will love Delco's chicken cheesesteak, which is wonderfully moist and flavorful, and every bit as good as the standard cheesesteak (some argue even better!). Delco's delivers for free, but like most grilled foodstuffs, there is no substitute for getting them fresh off the grill, moments after being heated and assembled, which explains why so many customers are regulars, and so many of the new customers become regulars, too. The interior is much like what you'd expect at a sandwich shop: racks of potato chips and packaged goodies along the wall, cheap tables and chairs, Pennsylvanian paraphernalia occupying much of the wall space, and more, but none of these things matters. It's what's going on the grill prior to landing in your basket. The cheesesteak at Delco's in Dunedin is one of the best in the Bay and is worth the drive for anyone jonesing for a taste of heaven from Philadelphia.

Eli's BBQ, 360 Skinner Blvd., Dunedin, FL 34698; (727) 738-4856; Barbecue; $. There is a man in a shack in Dunedin who makes some of the best barbecue in Tampa Bay. That man's name is Eli, and his restaurant is called Eli's BBQ and is open only two days a week. Eli's operation is entirely family-run, made with love and without cutting corners, in the simple and traditional method that was passed down to him from his family. Eli's opens at 11 a.m. every Fri and Sat and stays open until 6 p.m., or until they sell out of food (which they do nearly every week, so show up early). The menu is very simple (not that you'd expect it to be complicated) with sandwiches or dinner platters, homemade coleslaw and baked beans as the only options for sides, and pork, beef, sausage, chicken, and ribs the available choices of smoky delicious meat. Chopped pork is balanced and not too fatty but still quite tender, and ribs are the same, great smoke layer, tender meat, but not overly moist. No alcohol is available, only sodas and Gatorade, but given that there is very limited seating, it wouldn't be a half-bad idea to get food to go and take it a few hundred feet down the street to the air-conditioned **Dunedin Brewery** (p. 205) for a cold hand-crafted brew to wash down that meaty goodness.

Hellas, 735 Dodecanese Blvd., Tarpon Springs, FL 34689; (727) 945-7865; hellas-restaurant.com; Greek; $$$. Tarpon Springs has no shortage of Greek restaurants (actually it has a shortage of non-Greek restaurants, but that isn't necessarily a bad thing) all claiming to be the "most authentic" and have the "best Greek food." Truth is, most are good, and some are pretty great, while Hellas is pretty much the top dog. Hellas is among the largest of the Greek spots in Tarpon, with seating for well over 100 people, and one of the few Greek restaurants with a large bakery attached to it that (naturally) provides all its desserts. The bakery is a popular place to get an espresso or Greek coffee and a fresh baked baklava, while relaxing at one of their outdoor tables and watching the world go by. Hellas restaurant is one of the most ornately decorated on the interior, too; wooden tables are topped with hand-painted blue and white tiles, the ceiling is painted to look like the blue sky with clouds, blue rope accent lighting surrounds the room, wall murals are painted around the restaurant depicting scenes from Greece, and they even have a (rather gaudy) lit-up waterfall fountain in the middle of a wall, with various small statues and busts stuck on it. Far from classy but highly entertaining, it's as though Athens and Las Vegas had an illegitimate child and it grew up to be this building. Moving on, the food at Hellas is the star of the show and well worth the trip, and they even have some menu items not as commonly found at other local Greek eateries. A good variety of appetizers is available; if you're sharing with friends, the assorted cold plate is a great place to start with a variety of cold seafood and spreads, accompanied by olives, peppers, and cheese, or try the smoky and aromatic charbroiled marinated lamb riblets, with lemon and oregano. *Saganaki* is fun to order at any Greek restaurant; it's dinner with a show (imported cheese is lit on fire as the server yells "OPA!" and then extinguishes it with lemon juice, leaving the lemony caramelized soft cheese for diners to dig into). Only one soup is available, a classic Greek lemon and egg soup called *avgolemono*, and their fantastic Greek salad is not to miss, one of the best in Tarpon Springs. Kabobs, spring lamb, seafood, and other specialties make up the entree portion of the menu, and it's difficult to go wrong. Order your favorite or be adventurous: the spring lamb is considered a delicacy and isn't found at every Greek restaurant, though, so fans of lamb need look no further.

Henry's Chicago Beef and Dogs, 33135 US 19 N., Palm Harbor, FL 34684; (727) 785-7300; Cheesesteak/Hot Dogs/Sandwiches; $. Philadelphia has its beef sandwich (cheesesteak) and New York has its pizza. What does Chicago have? Both! Add in a definitive style of hot dog, and Chicago has a trifecta of comfort food that's hard to beat and bigger than the competition. That isn't to say Chicago's versions of these American staples are superior—crispy, thin NYC pizza is among the best pizza on the planet, and few things are more satisfying than a juicy Philly cheesesteak, but Chicago takes these things to a much more "filling" level. Henry's has what most Chicago natives consider to be the "closest thing to home" in the Bay area. Enter the Chicago beef (also known as the Italian beef), a powerhouse of a roast beef sandwich topped with giardineria (pickled veggies) and green Italian sweet peppers, and doused (sometimes dipped) in the beef jus. When executed with love and care, this sandwich can be one of the most delicious things you'll eat in a while. Whereas Chicago's deep-dish pizza is typically three times the heft of NY pizza, and the dogs are at least twice the weight, a Chicago beef is only slightly larger than a cheesesteak. Inside Henry's is clean and modern, with wood floors, accents, tables, and a large exposed stainless kitchen, an upscale sandwich shop feel to it. The Italian beef sandwiches and hot dogs are where Henry's shines; a big beefy dog is laid in a poppyseed bun and topped with neon-green relish, yellow mustard, red tomato, chopped onions, and pickled peppers, while the Italian beef is as meaty, messy, and delicious as any you'd have this side of Lake Michigan. Yum. Floridians and Chicago natives alike flock to Henry's on a regular basis and keep this Palm Harbor treasure busy day in and day out.

Hin Lee, 1757 Main St., Dunedin, FL 34698; (727) 736-3366; Sushi/Malaysian; $$. Malaysian food in Tampa Bay is a rare find; luckily, Hin Lee offers up a Malaysian menu in addition to its sushi and Chinese menus. OK, fair enough, Malaysia is hundreds if not thousands of miles away from both China and Japan, but most Floridians aren't familiar with Malaysian cuisine and there probably aren't enough Malaysian-American citizens living in Dunedin to keep a place with no "familiar" options available open for very long, so a restaurant must adapt. Fortunately for food lovers, Hin Lee adapted, and while less adventurous diners can nosh on sweet and sour pork or cashew chicken, the food lovers will be digging into a plate of Malaysian pork curry, mango shrimp, eggplant with black bean sauce, or beef rendang. Beef rendang is a unique and delicious dish, often described as a curry but truthfully nothing like a more familiar Western or Indian curry. Rendang is essentially a meat stewed in coconut milk and a dozen or so spices (ginger, lemongrass, shallot, chilies, galangal, and more) and is very time consuming to make, so it traditionally was served to honor people at ceremonies or to special guests. Although the hidden gem at Hin

Lee is the Malaysian grub, the sushi isn't half bad at all. There is a solid selection of fish on the nigiri menu (including conch, scallop, smoked oyster, mackerel, and quail egg) and some fun maki rolls, too. Food lovers on the hunt for something spicy and new should put Hin Lee on their short list immediately.

Island Way Grill, 20 Island Way, Clearwater, FL 33767; (727) 461-6617; islandwaygrill.com; Seafood/Brunch; $$$$. The view, the setting, the ambiance, and the location at Island Way Grill are hard to beat. Located just minutes from Clearwater Beach and from Downtown Clearwater lies a beautifully decorated, classy seafood restaurant perfect for impressing a date, a client, or just for digging on some great seafood. Stepping through the all-glass front doors (there's no shortage of glass in this restaurant, and that's a good thing) takes you into a lavish receiving area, with a large glass wine cellar along one wall across from a bar and bar tables, followed by travertine (there is beautiful natural stone wall and floor covering everywhere) and recessed wall pockets with beautiful, colorful large vases within. As you continue back into the dining area past the combination raw bar and sushi bar, a large window separating the main dining area and the back room sets a very aquatic mood given that the water cascading down it makes it look like a see-through waterfall. Naturally, the menu focuses on seafood, but a large portion of the menu is classic and contemporary preparations of land-dwelling animals, so diners not fond of seafood can still enjoy themselves and have a good variety of dishes to choose from. After selecting a bottle of wine from Island Way's fantastic wine selection (which has dozens of bottles, nearly all of which are priced from $25 to $70), start out your meal with a couple of sushi rolls, or try an appetizer like the Thai High Mussels (spicy, garlicky, and aromatic coconut milk broth with Thai basil) or go with the jalapeño conch fritters (spicy with a bit more bite and a great sweet chili dipping sauce). Entrees range from the more reasonable salmon *en papil-lote* (salmon cooked in parchment paper with Asian veggies and herbs) at $17 to the luxe Caribbean fire-roasted lobster tails (with wasabi mashed potatoes) for $40, and everything in between. Many regulars believe the best meal at Island Way Grill is the Sunday brunch, where dozens of different seafood dishes, sushi rolls, raw bar, desserts, and more are set up in stations around the restaurant in an eat-till-you-say-uncle configuration, a bargain given the view, atmosphere, and quality of food.

Kelly's For Just About Anything, 319 Main St., Dunedin, FL 34698; (727) 736-0206; kellyschicaboom.com; American/Breakfast; $$$. If they were to open a hotel adjacent to Kelly's, you could basically hang out all day. There would be no real reason to leave at all; this trio of buildings has a restaurant that serves breakfast (until 3 p.m.!), lunch, and dinner, attached to their martini bar called the Chic-a-Boom Room, which is attached to their nightclub called Blur. Throw in a large covered (and fan-cooled) outdoor patio surrounded by bamboo, live music, and bright, eclectic decor, and you've got one of the most fun places to be in Dunedin. The menu is equally fun and eclectic. Lunch is a great time to pick up one of Kelly's grilled brie sandwiches on sourdough with tomato and roasted garlic, or the practically fat-free Cajun bacon cheddar burger, voted one of the best burgers in the Bay and well worth every delicious calorie! Dinner is where the gloves really come off and Kelly's kicks it up a notch; a meal could be made of the appetizers alone. Start with the very dynamic house-made ravioli (stuffed with pickled fennel, carrots, bell peppers, and radish, finished with red coconut curry sauce and crumbled cashews) or the smoky, sweet, and rich smoked salmon egg roll with lemon dill cream cheese, napa cabbage, scallions, and honey horseradish sauce. If a sandwich is more your speed for dinner (and you brought your appetite), try the Beef Ridiculous, which is a heck of a sandwich with roast beef and corned beef stacked ridiculously high on rye, with a smear of horseradish mayo and Dijon mustard. If you're looking for a more meat-and-starch type entree, check out the sriracha pea-crusted Atlantic salmon on honey basil coulis pad thai noodles, or the Cornish game hen and baby back ribs combo, both house smoked, the hen with a maple pecan glaze and the ribs bathed in Alabama barbecue sauce. Come for dinner at Kelly's, stay for drinks at the Chic-a-Boom Room, and party the night away at Blur!

La Cabana del Tio, 1709 Drew St., Clearwater, FL 33755; (727) 466-0504; Mexican/Tacos; $. A tiny hole-in-the-wall Mexican spot for fantastic and authentic tacos, La Cabana Del Tio has more than a few people addicted to the fare. Aesthetically LCdT is nothing special, tucked in a tiny strip mall next to a Laundromat with nothing more than a sign in the window to identify it. Driving past it (more than once) is a common occurrence when trying to locate the place. Inside there is enough seating for a dozen people or so, and no real decor to speak of, making it a popular spot more for take-out than dine-in. The menu is also rather limited, but that's probably a good thing—the cooks can focus on making the from-scratch salsas and sauces, and grilling up some of the best tacos around. *Carnitas* (pork) is popular and thought to be one of the best meat choices for the tacos by the regulars (addicts), and tacos are served up authentically with onion, cilantro, and lime on house-made corn tortillas. *Gorditas* are another strong dish at La Cabana, crunchy and topped with refried beans and *queso fresco* (crumbly Mexican cheese), while beans and rice make a great side and are served in a rather large portion (more than enough to share). What the restaurant lacks in looks, it makes up for in spades with some of the best Mexican food around.

The Living Room, 487 Main St., Dunedin, FL 34698; (727) 736-5202; thelivingroomonmain.com; Tapas; $$$. It is not an uncommon occurrence in Tampa Bay to find a restaurant that was once a home decades prior, with a proprietor who has spent considerable time and money making the interior of the building look more like a restaurant and less like a domicile. The Living Room on Main Street in Dunedin did just the opposite; they took a building and made it look more like a living room, just as the name would lead you to believe. Drapes and curtains, columns and doorways, faux finishes, paintings, lamps, and bookshelves all add to the feel of being at a lively (often packed) dinner party, and a party it is. The Living Room has a happening bar scene and frequently features live music! The bar and the band aren't the only entertaining things at the restaurant—the menu is pretty exciting, too. Chef Tony Bruno put together a menu of small and large tapas-size portions, mostly of Mediterranean origin, with a bit of American and Asian influence mixed in for flavor. The portions make for a fantastic sampling and sharing menu, so bringing friends is always a good idea, although two or three small dishes might make a very satisfying meal for someone flying solo. Wild mushroom grilled flatbread pizza or the mango brie quesadilla are great share dishes to begin the meal, or go for Chef Bruno's Tapas Plate, which changes daily and uses whatever is fresh and seasonal. Diners trying to watch their figures while still eating something delicious will be excited to see the variety of salads on TLR's menu, from the creamy and tart Insalata Olympia to the sweet and crunchy Asian pear salad. Moving into something more meaty, hoisin-glazed pork shanks are slow braised and served with a side of spicy cucumber kimchi, while the bayou jumbo shrimp have a bit more of a citrus kick given that they are sautéed in lemon, Worcestershire, and white wine, but are well complemented by the creamy Gouda grit cakes they're served on. Much of the menu is excellent, so try a variety of dishes, enjoy the music and the atmosphere, relax, and have fun!

The Lucky Dill Deli, 33180 US 19 N., Palm Harbor, FL 34683; (727) 789-5574; luckydilldeli.com; American/Sandwiches/Salads; $$. On most days there is practically a line out the door to get in to the Lucky Dill Deli for one of their pastrami sandwiches, which they jokingly claim is "the sandwich that ate Brooklyn" on the cover of their menu. Although deli fare is what the restaurant is best known for, the Dill also offers an extensive breakfast menu (with omelets, scrambles, poached eggs, french toast, pancakes, waffles, even naan pizzas) and a late-night menu with everything from flatbread pizzas to sliders. The restaurant became so popular it moved from its original location on Alternate US 19 to the larger current space, expanding and adding a cocktail lounge called the "NYC Bar and Tribeca Lounge," which has turned the restaurant into a popular nightlife hangout, too. The cocktail menu at the bar and lounge is as extensive as the food menu, with multiple variations on drinks like mojitos, Manhattans, and more.

Marley's Monster Grill & Pizza, 29835 US 19 N., Clearwater, FL 33761; (727) 239-7208; marleysmonstergrill.com; Burgers/Pizza/Seafood; $$. Owners Pop-pop and Granny (Alan and Jacqui Bredt) planned on opening a restaurant in Philadelphia but instead chose to come down to Florida to be closer to family and named Marley's Monster Grill after their grandson, Marley. Fortunately for everyone in Florida, they chose us over the good people of Pennsylvania and brought with them what very well may be the best Philly cheesesteak in town. Oh man, that cheesesteak, a thing of beauty. It would stand up to most steaks from the motherland (Philadelphia), and it's available here in Clearwater! Alan and Jacqui chose to create a better-quality product rather than maximize their profit margins when it came to selecting ingredients for the sandwich: great cheese, high-quality shaved rib eye, good onions and mushrooms, and that soft, fresh, lightly toasted 12-inch Amoroso's roll—heaven. It's difficult to want to order anything other than the Philly, but don't be afraid to explore the rest of the menu. Marley's wings are meaty and excellent, made to order (wet or dry, well done or regular, etc.), the pizza is darn tasty, even the onion rings are perfectly seasoned and not over-breaded. The owners and cooks at Marley's seem to have put love into each menu item, and few visitors don't return a second, third, and fourth time to sample their simple and delicious grub.

Mezze on Main, 680 Main St., Dunedin, FL 34698; (727) 216-6222; mezzeonmain.com; Mediterranean; $$$. Formerly Cafe DePaz, Mezze on Main is one of Dunedin's best Mediterranean restaurants with an energetic atmosphere, live music, and a rockin' small plates menu. Chef-Owner David DePaz created a menu that explores food from multiple countries across the Mediterranean (Greece, Italy,

Spain, Israel, and more) and even includes some darn good pizzas (the mushroom pie alone is worth the visit) cooked in the restaurant's brick oven. A good variety of entrees is available (steaks, lamb chops, salmon, and more), but these almost seem to be a tactical error given that the level of creativity in the tapas-size plates makes for a more interesting meal, coupled with the fact diners can try a greater variety of dishes when ordering small plates, providing an opportunity to explore more of the menu. Chef DePaz is actually from Israel, where he was a restaurant owner prior to moving to the USA, bringing his love of food and his experience with worldly cuisine to cozy Dunedin, Florida. Meals start out with complimentary flatbread and a side of feta and olives in olive oil that are salty and rich, and really make the bread pop. A great first course would be a brick-oven pizza, or perhaps a cheese plate; Chef DePaz has an excellent knowledge of cheeses, and correspondingly the restaurant has a fantastic selection to offer, typically showing up with some jam, bread, and other complements. Keep an eye on the specials board for food, wine, and cocktail specials, and to find out who the next live musician will be—the space has a fantastic setup for singers or groups to entertain diners. Covered outdoor dining is also available, although the ambiance of the interior decor is lost, along with the air-conditioning, which may be a good or bad thing depending on what time of year it is.

Mykonos, 628 Dodecanese Blvd., Tarpon Springs, FL 34689; (727) 934-4306; Greek; $$. One of Tarpon Springs's most loved Greek restaurants is Mykonos. A white building with blue awnings, doors, shutters, and trim (to match the colors of the Grecian flag, naturally), Mykonos serves up some great and authentic Greek food in the middle of Tarpon Springs right off Dodecanese Boulevard. Tarpon Springs is a really fun place to visit when in the Tampa Bay area; unique culture, shopping, scenery, and best of all, food is plentiful in this small but great city, and the locals make up the highest Greek concentration of any community in the entire country! Start your meal with a palate-opening Greek salad, the mixture of crunch from the green peppers, lettuce, and onions balancing the slight saltiness of the feta cheese and olives, and the rich, smooth character of the olive oil. A *skaras* plate makes a great meaty appetizer for the table. Mykonos offers selections from both land and sea—the *mezethakia skaras* comes with charbroiled *soutzoukakia* (ground beef and greek herbs), pork souvlaki, chicken souvlaki, and gyro meat, while the *thallasina skaras* has charbroiled shrimp, octopus, and kalamaria. Entrees at Mykonos are a meat-eater's delight—does ground beef and macaroni in a creamy cheese sauce baked and topped with grated cheese sound good? Go with the *pastitsio*. Or try the lamb *youvetsi*, baked in a clay pot with tomato sauce, lamb, cheese, orzo pasta, and more deliciousness than you can shake a fork at. Local fresh catch is also available, charbroiled or pan fried, and with a bit of salt, pepper, lemon, and olive oil, it's a great way to taste some of the best from the Bay!

Mystic Fish, 3253 Tampa Rd., Palm Harbor, FL 34684; (727) 771-1800; 3bestchefs.com; Seafood; $$$. Sister restaurant to Indian Rocks Beach hot spot **Guppy's** (p. 153), Mystic Fish brings great seafood to the Palm Harbor area in an attractive and inviting space. You'll walk through the colorful stained-glass front door, a fitting entrance, and the decor matches the colorful food and vibrant character of the restaurant and sets a jovial mood to what is typically a very enjoyable meal. Chef Doug Bebell and co-owners/partners were successful in bringing good seafood to Tampa Bay in the early 1990s with Guppy's and wanted to bring that same caliber of seafood to the Palm Harbor area, so nearly a decade later Mystic Fish was born. The menu at Mystic Fish is primarily American, focused on seafood, with a number of European and Asian influences scattered throughout. The chef does a good job of keeping "something for everyone" available. Small plates are a great place to start, such as the herbed goat cheese spring rolls with fig balsamic glacé and artichoke tapenade, or the maple leaf duck breast with apricot-curry sauce and sliced strawberries. Both dishes have great elements of spice, rich, sweet, and bright flavors to create a satisfying start to a meal. Daily specials change frequently but have included special and less common fish such as panko-crusted hogfish with soy beurre blanc and wakami salad, or swordfish Diane with beech mushrooms and Dijon-Worcestershire sauce. The selection of beer and wine at Mystic Fish seems to be well thought out; many different styles and varietals are available to pair with the numerous different dishes, and at very reasonable prices, too. Bottles of wine start at less than $20 (but worry not, wine lovers, they have the high-end juice too) and craft beer around $4. Mystic Fish also has a full liquor bar if spirits are your thing, and friendly bartenders are quick to mix up a specialty cocktail or two.

Ohana Cafe, 306 Orange St. N., Palm Harbor, FL 34683; (727) 787-1234; theohanacafe.com; Hawaiian; $$. Aloha! Welcome to the only restaurant in the Bay area that offers free hugs. Ohana Cafe is a family-run establishment (*ohana* is the Hawaiian word for family) that is truthfully unlike any other. The space is very laid-back and a dead ringer for a casual restaurant in Hawaii, only transplanted to the quaint community of Ozona. Upon entering, you are likely to be greeted by a woman named Teresa who has a big welcoming smile (and possibly pigtails) and will happily show you to your seat and tell you a bit about the restaurant if it's your first visit. Ohana's focus was creating a menu that was healthy and organic with vegan and gluten-free options available, all without sacrificing flavor, and they've accomplished exactly that. Carnivores shouldn't read that and be concerned; Ohana offers a number of dishes with meat, including one of their most popular, the Loco Moco Bowl (brown rice topped with an organic buffalo patty, a fried egg, sautéed onions, and covered in gravy). Another fantastic option for meat eaters is the sweet and salty Honolulu Ham Sandwich, with nitrate-free ham, pineapple, provolone, asparagus, and sweet onion, offered on ciabatta or organic wheat bread. It's difficult to believe eating healthy can taste so good, and as if having healthy food that is actually flavorful weren't enough, Ohana has live hula dancers on weekends, so diners can get a show to go with their grub. A solid selection of quality beer and wine is available, and the list naturally leans toward selections that are organic or sustainably made. Guilt-free food, the most welcoming atmosphere imaginable, and dinner with a show make Ohana Cafe an easy recommendation to make for anyone in the area!

Parts of Paris Bistro, 146 4th Ave. N., Safety Harbor, FL 34695; (727) 797-7979; partsofparis.com; French; $$$. Parts of Paris Bistro, a newer establishment in downtown Safety Harbor, breathed a bit more life into the mostly pedestrian dining scene of the small community. Elegant in its simplicity, PoP put considerable effort into creating a very viable concept and has clearly succeeded. There is a feeling of composure throughout the menu, the dining space, the decor, the service, and the execution. Start with decor—espresso-colored wood makes up floors, shelving, chairs, and the bar, while all else (with the exception of a couple accent walls) is white. Ceilings, walls, tablecloths, chair cushions, lights, outdoor planters, all white. The sharp contrast of dark vs. light, coupled with a minimal amount of any additional decoration, actually makes for a very clean, modern, attractive space. The menu is equally clean and simple: six apps, two soups, nine entrees, and four desserts, composed neatly on one page, and impressively enough nothing feels as though it is missing. Appetizers range from light (salad niçoise with tuna, anchovies, egg, *haricots verts,* mesclun) to heavy (*foie gras* with artisan bread and roasted peaches), while both the soups are on the heartier side; this is French cooking after all. The Bistro offers a number of classic entrees, such as filet au poivre, a filet mignon in a creamy peppercorn sauce, or *canard a l'orange*, a seared duck breast with orange marmalade, or even the classic bouillabaisse, their version with lobster, sea bass, mussels, clams, and shrimp. Desserts are simple, traditional, and good: the crème brûlée is silky and elegant, tarte tatin is sweet, slightly tart, and the mixture of hot pastry and cold ice cream makes for a great combination of flavors. Parts of Paris is a welcome addition to Safety Harbor and is well worth a visit.

Pinocchio's Pizza Restaurant, 35236 US 19 N., Palm Harbor, FL 34684; (727) 785-1400; pinocchiospizzeria.com; Pizza; $$. Should you find yourself in Palm Harbor and hungry for good New York–style pizza, head over to Pinocchio's Pizza Restaurant on US 19. Formerly known as Aiello's, Pinocchio's Chef-Owner Charlie Aiello brought his love of (and ninja-like talent for making) pizza to Florida from the Empire State, where he owned a pizza shop making pies for the most discerning of customers: New Yorkers. Although pizza is clearly Aiello's specialty, the menu is more than just a one-trick pony: Garlic knots and pasta dishes like cheese manicotti and homemade lasagna are very popular with the regulars, and calzones and strombolis are well-seasoned, cheese-filled treats. Charlie himself is often in the kitchen, tossing the dough, ladling the sauce, spreading the cheese, and his faithful followers appreciate him for it. Pinocchio's is a neighborhood favorite for Palm Harbor residents hungry for good pizza and pasta and is a welcome find for New Yorkers visiting or transplanted to Florida.

Plaka, 769 Dodecanese Blvd., Tarpon Springs, FL 34689; (727) 934-4752; plakatarponsprings.com; Greek; $$. Tarpon Springs is a city in northern Pinellas County that is famous for its sponge docks (it was a major producer of sponge in the early half of the twentieth century) and also famous for having the highest concentration of Greek citizens in the United States. Given that it's a very tourist-visited area, naturally a lot of touristy Greek restaurants have sprung up, and hungry visitors often want to know which restaurants serve the best and most authentic Greek food of them all. Plaka is one of the more authentic, especially when it comes to the gyro. A gyro is sea-soned beef and lamb cooked on a rotisserie and sliced into a pita, with lettuce and tomato, and a yogurt-like sauce called tzatziki. Most restaurants today don't go through the hassle of making their own gyro meat, as it is such a time-consuming process, so frequently what is served is a mass-produced compressed ground meat "loaf" that is easy to purchase and put onto the rotisserie. Plaka, on the other hand, still hand-makes their gyro meat, and even house-makes their tzatziki sauce, too (many restaurants just use store-bought sauce), which many residents of Tarpon Springs and of Tampa Bay in general consider to be the best-tasting gyro around. Although Plaka does a fantastic job with the gyros, that's not the only item on the menu worth trying. Their special Greek salad is a filling portion of a healthy mix of veggies and legumes, cheese, and even anchovies should you desire (which you should). Souvlaki (kebobs) are marinated and spiced, available in pork, lamb, and chicken, and recommended as a complement to a gyro, which makes for a hearty and delicious meal. The decor, ambiance, wine and beer list, and location aren't anything to brag about (it's a bit of a homely hole-in-the-wall), but a trip to Plaka should be for the love of food and nothing else.

Rumba Island Bar & Grill, 1800 Gulf to Bay Blvd., Clearwater, FL 33765; (727) 446-7027; rumbaislandgrill.com; Seafood/Barbecue/Caribbean; $$$. "Eat, Drink, Party" is the mantra at Rumba Island, a popular Caribbean restaurant on Gulf to Bay Boulevard in Clearwater created by the same restaurant group that cooked up **Island Way Grill** (p. 171) and **Salt Rock Grill** (p. 157), two other great Pinellas County seafood spots. Rumba Island's menu is also seafood-centric, and Chef DC Chambers (a native of Jamaica) isn't afraid to get liberal with the spices and seasonings. Decor is simple and clean, convivial without being hokey, and the outdoor seating and tiki bar space are great for al fresco dining. Exploring the menu is fun, and selecting what to eat may be difficult given that there are so many yummy options. Crunchy and citrusy conch ceviche or conch fritters aren't a bad place to start though, or perhaps some sweet and tangy cranberry jerk chicken wings. Getting deeper into the menu affords diners additional tasty options. Coconut-crusted mahi has a great mix of flavors, topped with a jalapeño aioli and pineapple sauce and accompanied by a pair of sides (although adding the house crab mac n' cheese is highly recommended). If you're not in the mood for seafood, try the island grilled meat loaf with onions and peppers; it's like meat loaf your mother used to make you, assuming your mother was a Jamaican guy named DC Chambers. The restaurant runs a number of drink specials, and although the wine and beer list is rather simple, the prices are very reasonable. Rum lovers are in for a treat, as a "rum atlas" is available with numerous selections ranging from affordable to very high end. One of the better restaurants in Clearwater, Rumba Island is the place to go for well-seasoned food and a good time.

Rusty Bellies Waterfront Restaurant, 937 Dodecanese Blvd., Tarpon Springs, FL 34689; (727) 934-4047; rustybellies.com; Seafood; $$. Rusty Bellies is a family-friendly Florida seafood spot with a view. Rusty isn't a foodie mecca and doesn't advertise to be one either. They do, however, crank out some fresh-caught fried, grilled, and blackened local seafood every day to hundreds of hungry locals. Located right on the water with boats continuously sailing by, the restaurant provides a perfect example of what a classic Florida seafood restaurant looks and feels like: sticky menus, wood everywhere, inexpensive tables and plates, nothing special on the wine or beer menu, just good food. Upon being seated, diners are brought a paper bag with hush puppies in it, a fitting start to the meal and a great bite-size snack to quiet noisy stomachs prior to ordering. Menu choices have hokey names (naturally) such as the Madame Butterfly (butterflied shrimp) or the Early Out (fresh mullet, fried), or even the Johnny O (local grouper or mahi fried, grilled, or blackened). Fried or blackened seafood is the go-to dish here and trying as many different items as possible is the way to eat; fortunately, that isn't difficult given the numerous combo selections on the menu. Show up at Rusty Bellies with a desire for nothing more than tasty local seafood, and you should leave quite satisfied.

Serendipity Cafe, 664 Main St., Dunedin, FL 34698; (727) 483-9233; myserendipitycafe.com; American/Organic; $. Dunedin's Serendipity Cafe has an inexpensive menu that is appealing to food-lovers, diners with gluten allergies, and herbivores alike. The cafe serves meat, worry not, my meat-loving friends, but they also offer soups, salads, dips, smoothies, pizzas, and wraps, all delicious and meat free, and healthy to boot. Breakfast is served "all day long" (well, until they close around 3 p.m.; Serendipity is more of a before-dinner spot) and has offerings of cornmeal pancakes with almonds and blueberry syrup, Cameron's heavenly french toast with organic peanut butter syrup and grilled banana, and a pretty killer breakfast bowl with hormone-free chicken andouille sausage sprinkled over free range eggs and veggies, piled on brown rice. Smoothies are much more fun than your typical pedestrian selections. Serendipity's menu offers vanilla chai, green monster, chocolate monkey, and one that is clearly healthy called Antioxidants Rock. Hummus makes a great starter, as do kale chips (try mixing the two together for experimental awesomeness), and soups are made from scratch every day. The Asian kale salad sounds like one of the healthiest and tastiest things on the menu, with kale, red peppers, carrots, roasted pumpkin seeds, and a ginger sesame tamari dressing. Pizzas are fewer to choose from (although diners could always custom build their own), although the Gramma's Loaded Pizza is the kitchen sink of veggie pizzas with organic spinach, zucchini, mushrooms, artichoke hearts, tomato, and a sprinkle of cheese and red sauce on a brown rice tortilla. Serendipity's wraps are great and have multiple meat and non-meat offerings, and nearly everything on the entire menu is less than $10, so a trip to this yummy little cafe will be as good for your budget as it is for your health!

Food Trucks

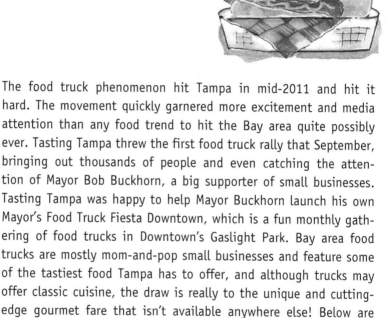

The food truck phenomenon hit Tampa in mid-2011 and hit it hard. The movement quickly garnered more excitement and media attention than any food trend to hit the Bay area quite possibly ever. Tasting Tampa threw the first food truck rally that September, bringing out thousands of people and even catching the attention of Mayor Bob Buckhorn, a big supporter of small businesses. Tasting Tampa was happy to help Mayor Buckhorn launch his own Mayor's Food Truck Fiesta Downtown, which is a fun monthly gathering of food trucks in Downtown's Gaslight Park. Bay area food trucks are mostly mom-and-pop small businesses and feature some of the tastiest food Tampa has to offer, and although trucks may offer classic cuisine, the draw is really to the unique and cutting-edge gourmet fare that isn't available anywhere else! Below are just a few of the fantastic food trucks rolling around the streets of Tampa Bay. For the latest info on where to find the trucks and what food truck rallies are going on, keep an eye on facebook.com/tampabayfoodtruckrally.

American Weiner, facebook.com/wienertruck; Hot Dogs. When Chef Kevin Dunn started his food truck, he knew he had to have a winning concept, so he decided to take a popular food everyone already loved and elevate it to a more "gourmet" level, and American Weiner was born. Not just hot dogs, but high-end dogs with creative toppings like the Japanese-themed dog with ginger, shredded nori, sesame seeds, and wasabi mayo, or the *merguez* (lamb sausage), which is delicious all by itself but gets chef's creative toppings of the week to make it even better. Fans of hot dogs will love this creative and inexpensive take on an American classic; as Chef Kevin says, remember to "eat more wieners!"

Bayou Bistro, facebook.com/CurbsideBayouBistro; Twitter: @ BayouBistro; Cajun/Creole. There is a very cleverly decorated food truck (propane tanks that look like Tabasco bottles, talking alligators, etc.) on the Tampa scene whipping up some peppery Cajun goodness that's causing quite a buzz, and it's called Bayou Bistro. Catfish Taceaux, oyster po'boys, gumbo, red beans and rice, boudin balls, and shrimp and grits are just a few of the things BB is bringing to the table, and each is seasoned and spicy enough to be worthy of its Louisiana heritage. For diners who have never had the opportunity to try them, boudin balls are fritter-size fried balls of sausage and rice that have a wonderfully soft texture inside, a nice lightly crisp exterior shell, and are jam-packed with flavor. Though the boudin balls are amazing, possibly the best item on the truck is the Catfish Taceaux (tacos), with moist blackened catfish, seasoned liberally with Cajun heat, and cooled down a bit by a creamy pickled slaw that pairs beautifully with the spices. Tampa is blessed to have some wonderful food trucks, and Bayou Bistro is a welcome addition to the growing armada.

Burger Culture, burgerculturetruck.com; Twitter: @Burger Culture1; Hamburgers. What is more American than a hamburger? Not much, but even if these seasoned and juicy patties were from Kazakhstan, chances are good that Burger Culture would still be one of the most popular food trucks in the Bay area. Burger Culture Owners Gabe and Ashley are vets of the service industry (they were coworkers from seafood mecca **Oystercatchers** [p. 107]); both loved a good burger and saw a gap that needed filling in Tampa's food truck scene and decided to jump on the opportunity. BC offers nearly a dozen different burgers, from the basic (yet still tasty) beef burger for the less adventurous, to lamb, kobe, and bison for people wanting to pay a couple extra bucks for the good stuff. The Cajun burger is particularly awesome, smothered in mushrooms, cheddar cheese, and dripping with "Chipotle Secret Love Sauce," as local blogger Bill Leon described it. Truly one of the best burgers in town—this truck is worth the drive to wherever they're serving lunch to check it out.

DaKine Hawaiian Cafe, dakinehc.com; Twitter: @DaKineHC; Hawaiian. Not often mobile, but a definite Tampa favorite, DaKine is a Hawaiian food truck that is currently stationed at the Harley Davidson dealership on North Dale Mabry (north of Sligh Avenue) and has a simple but effective menu of Owner Steve Clay's favorites from the islands. The Loco Moco Burger is an island staple, covered in brown gravy and topped with a fried egg, that will cure just about any hunger (or hangover) known to man. The crowd favorite seems to be the Da-Combo, a plate (Styrofoam box) of DaKine's three meats: Hawaiian steak, shoyu chicken, and Issa's sweet ribs. The combo comes with rice, and a side of the infamous DaKine peppery macaroni salad, which (insider secret) is fantastic when drizzled with sriracha hot sauce. If taking food to go, make sure not to miss their house-made "Da-Sauce," which is essentially a thin, sweet soy sauce that goes really well with the rice, steak, and chicken.

Dochos, facebook.com/pages/Dochos-Concession; Sandwiches/ Desserts. Like many food truck owners, Debbie Guy had both a passion and a day job. She and her husband saved up enough money to buy a food truck, and initially fried up fun carnival food such as fried Oreos or funnel cakes, which are quite popular at food truck events, but they wanted to grow beyond that. Enter the Monte Castro. Debbie makes a killer Cuban sandwich (which would honestly stand up to, if not beat, most in Tampa) with her own juicy and tender roast pork and an excellent ratio of sliced meats to pickles to mustard, etc. The Cuban all by itself is fantastic, but what if it were fried like a Monte Cristo sandwich? Would the Monte Castro be amazing or too much? It certainly isn't a dainty food item, but words do it no justice. It is a sandwich you'll never forget. A crispy shell gives way to toasted pressed Cuban bread for two layers of crunch (and the bread inside doesn't get greasy), and then the saltiness of the meats, the kick of the mustard, the clean bite of the pickles—it's just fantastic. Track them down and try one.

Fat Tortillas, facebook.com/FatTortillas; Twitter: @FatTortillas; Tex/Mex. Another husband-and-wife team, Glenn and Heidi Nagle started up their food truck Fat Tortillas and hit the ground running in mid-2011, participating in the first Tampa Food Truck Rally, where they sold out of their tasty burritos, quesadillas, tacos, and nachos in just over an hour. Fat Tortillas mixes up fresh Tex-Mex and has been a staple of the Tampa food truck scene since the very beginning.

Graffeaties, graffeaties.blogspot.com; Twitter: @graffEATIES; International. A newer food truck to the Tampa scene, Graffeaties serves up international street food in a fun and colorful truck, wrapped to look like a brick wall covered in (wait for it . . .) graffiti. Owners Natalie Spencer and Brent Tenzel were high school friends who met back up at Natalie's bar in North Tampa and were both so enticed by the food truck craze that they decided to have their own, but wanted to do something unique, and do it right. They clearly succeeded—the food is excellent and everyone loves the truck! A couple of the not-to-miss items are the Hawaii 5-0 sandwich (fried Spam patty topped with fried egg, napa cabbage, and tomato jam on a Hawaiian roll, pressed until crispy) and the Brazilian hot dog (cooked in marinara and topped with onion/tomato relish, garlic mashed potatoes, and potato sticks with an aioli drizzle). Outstanding.

Jimmy Meatballs, facebook.com/JimmyMeatballs; Italian. These are without question some of the best meatballs in all of Tampa Bay. Jimmy Meatballs has a fantastic concept: cool-looking truck, very reasonable price point (most items between $3 and $6), a sampler for indecisive people or those looking for variety, and sliders or hoagies if a sandwich is desired. The meatballs are super moist and tender, and come in a variety of flavors, Korean barbecue being one of the favorites (sweet pork meatballs with red chili sauce over mojo slaw). The classic meatballs (called "Granma's Classic") are also excellent, a perfectly seasoned beef/pork blend, topped with tomato sauce and cheese. Dessert wasn't forgotten—JM offers a Death by Chocolate Ball, a pretty decadent and delicious fried cake ball with brownie and Nutella inside and drizzled in chocolate sauce. Jimmy's is a real hit wherever they go, so if you're visiting them at a food truck rally, make sure to get there early to beat the lines!

Keep'n It Reel, facebook.com/pages/Keepn-It-Reel; Twitter: @Keep_nItReel; Seafood. Richard Calvecca loved to fish (as many Floridians do) and had a heck of a knack for cooking up his fresh catch for himself and his friends. There are only so many times someone can be told "This is so amazing, you MUST go into business for yourself!" about their food before they make a plan and set sail on their own small-business adventure, which is exactly what Richard did with his food truck Keep'n It Reel.

While Florida law mandates that Richard can't cook up the fish he catches personally, he still sources some great quality seafood, as much locally caught as possible, and really knocks some of his dishes out of the park. Richard's mahi tacos are fantastic, with tender, seasoned mahi and a spicy sweet pineapple wasabi slaw. At $3 there are few better fish tacos to be had in this town. Key West pink shrimp make for a mean buffalo shrimp po'boy, with lettuce, tomato, and pickles, and jalapeño hush puppies are the perfect crunchy and spicy complement to any dish. Some of the best seafood in Tampa can only be found using Facebook and Twitter, so keep an eye out on "line"!

Mike's Off the Hook, facebook.com/MikesOffTheHook; Twitter: @MIKESOFFTHEHOOK; Seafood. Floridians love their seafood. The state is filled with locals and tourists alike that take advantage of fishing off our hundreds of miles of beautiful coastline and excitedly seek out the best seafood in the area when not cooking their own. Mike's Off the Hook is a mobile seafood vendor that serves fresh and cleverly named dishes at a great price point. Some treats from his menu include the "Tally Ho," a crispy fish filet drizzled with tartar sauce and covered with salt 'n' vinegar chips served on a brioche bun, and the very popular "Hogan's Hero," a blackened fish filet with baby swiss cheese, sauerkraut, and zesty sauce served on grilled pumpernickel and rye swirled bread. Mike's is definitely worth "catching" if you can!

Renny's Oki Doki, facebook.com/RennysOkiDoki; Twitter: @RennysOkiDoki; Japanese. Ask Renny Braga how he's doing and he'll excitedly shout "Oki doki!" as he prepares some of the most delicious Okinawan food in town for fans of his food truck. Renny and his wife run the Oki Doki truck, and together they whip up goodies such as *chuka soba* (cold soba noodles, veggies, chives, egg, bean sprouts), pork belly fried rice, rafute wraps (with pork belly, rice, and veggies), spicy habu wings, and more. Renny's story is an interesting one: He wanted to share his love for Okinawan food with Tampa Bay but didn't have the money to finish building his food truck, so he turned to crowd funding via the website kickstarter.com and uploaded a video telling his story and describing his cuisine. Miraculously in a very short amount of time people pledged the thousands necessary to get Oki Doki up and running, and Renny quickly finished building his truck, immediately threw a big party to celebrate, and invited all the people who helped fund the truck. Authentic Okinawan food is rare in Tampa, so give Renny's a shot; you'll be happy you did!

Rollin Zoinks, facebook.com/RollinZoinksTruck; Twitter: @RollinZoinks; American. What is a "Zoink"? Owner Tammy Young was kind enough to define it right on her food truck. The word can mean a number of things, but in this case it refers to a handheld food wrap that comes stuffed with ingredient combinations yummy enough that they'd make Scooby and Shaggy come running. One of the most popular Zoinks is The Southerner, which is essentially your grandma's home-cooked meal stuffed into a wrap. It comes with fried chicken, green beans, risotto, cheddar cheese, roasted corn, and buttermilk bacon gravy. Yes, please! Tammy's seafood offering is also great, The Scallywag, which is delightfully stuffed with seared scallops, snow peas, couscous, mushrooms, Parmesan, and a bright tangy lemon champagne sauce. Diners may be asking themselves what a Zoink is, but that usually only lasts until they eat one, at which point the lingering question becomes, "Where and when can I get another one?"

Stinky Bunz, stinkybunz.com; Twitter: @Stinky_Bunz; Korean. Restaurant veteran husband-and-wife team Xuan (pronounced "Sing") and Kevin Hurt are a fantastic young couple with a love for food. Xuan is of Asian descent and a killer cook, while Kevin is American as apple pie and a huge foodie. They were a match made in heaven that all the citizens of Tampa Bay get to benefit from, as they're sharing their fantastic food with people all over the Bay. Stinky Bunz runs special dishes frequently, but they are best known for their Steamed Bunz, a handheld bun with kimchi slaw, lettuce, cilantro, and one of a variety of meats, or with tofu for veggie lovers. People watching their carbs can opt for the lettuce wraps, which are much like the buns but served in a leaf of lettuce—healthy and delicious! See Chef Xuan's recipes for **Lemongrass Pork Patties, Cucumber Kimchi,** and **Fresh Apple Slaw** starting on p. 216.

Tasty Stacy, tastystacyfoodtruck.com; Twitter: @Tasty_Stacy; Italian. Rob and Stacy Rizzo turned their love of cooking and love of food into a small business called the Tasty Stacy Food Truck, dishing up tasty Italian-American food everywhere their wheels take them. Stacy has a big presence on the truck or out greeting customers to take their orders, always a big welcoming smile and plenty of delicious recommendations for what to order off the menu. Sandwiches are always a safe bet, and Stacy's Italian sausage sandwich with Parmesan or the caprese sandwich with baby mozzarella, basil, tomato, and balsamic are always safe bets for tasty food. The true can't-miss item on Stacy's truck though isn't a sandwich or pasta dish; it's her homemade chocolate chip cookies! Gooey chocolate chunks (often with white chocolate chips mixed in for extra delicious-ness) make this buttery soft cookie one of the best around; it's worth every penny.

2 Asians and A Grill, 2asians1grill.com; Twitter:@2asians1grill; Japanese. James Lee's food truck was an immediate hit in Tampa, serving up hibachi favorites, sushi, appetizers like steamed buns and egg rolls, and other Asian favorites to hungry citizens. Nothing crazy or exotic, just good food, fresh and well prepared. The 2 Asians crew will bring a hibachi grill anywhere and set up right outside their truck! This makes them quite popular at parties and lunch events, although they typically don't do so at food truck rallies because it's time consuming and would end up bottlenecking orders. If you're in the mood for Asian comfort food, this is the way to go.

Unforgettable Cupcakes, unforgettablecupcakes.net; Twitter: @unforgetcupcake; Desserts. Surprise! We have another great example of a mom-and-pop start-up where a couple's love for food was able to bridge the gap from dream to reality thanks to the relative affordability of food trucks. Owners Juan and Shirley outfitted their cupcake truck with enough racks to hold hundreds of their delicious made-from-scratch cupcakes, and the couple has agreed on their duties: Juan drives the truck and sells the 'cakes, and Shirley bakes and works on new flavor combinations and recipes. While flavors like Lemon Drop, Red Velvet, Cookies n' Creamy, and Peanut Butter Dynamite are all delicious, the most unforgettable of all the cupcakes UC sells is by far the Maple Bacon cupcake. Sweet and creamy, but just a bit smoky and salty, the Maple Bacon cupcake is usually the first one to disappear at events, and rightfully so—it's a delight for the senses.

Whatever Pops, whateverpops.com; Twitter: @WhateverPops; Desserts. Steve McGlocklin visited a particularly impressive gourmet ice pop shop in St. Augustine, Florida, on a trip and fell in love. Shortly after leaving, he decided to cook up some of his own recipes and share the love of all-natural, additive-free, gourmet ice pops with the Tampa Bay area, and God bless the man for it. At most food truck rallies, Steve can be found doling out his wares at $3 a pop (literally), with amazing flavors like Coconut Lime, Earl Grey Lavender, Riesling Pear, Chocolate Sea Salt, Caramel Coffee, and many more. All handmade by Steve himself, and all additive-free, these aren't grocery store pops. The depth and layers of flavor in these frozen delights take the ice pop to a whole new level and make store-bought pops seem bland and over-sweetened by comparison. Steve has a cart and a decades-old mail truck he converted into his pop-mobile that he takes to rallies and other events. Hit him up early at any event as he sells out of the most popular flavors pretty quickly. There really is no more delicious way to beat the heat.

Wicked 'Wiches, wickedwiches.com; Twitter: @Wicked_Wiches; Sandwiches. Wicked 'Wiches hit the scene in 2011 and really stirred up the food truck craze in Tampa Bay. They were the first of the trucks in town to have a big custom-made truck with a pretty wrap, blinking lights, the whole nine yards. The truck is owned by Brian Goodell (who also owns **Fresh Restaurant** [p. 50] in downtown Tampa), a man with an eye for creative food. The menu changes frequently and features primarily sandwiches (well, duh), but they're sandwiches that you may not find anywhere else in town. Two particularly excellent offerings typically available are their Cuban Philly (a marriage of two fantastic sandwiches that you'll immediately be addicted to) and the Monte Cristo du jour, which is seasonal or off the cuff; Thanksgiving's was turkey with cranberry jelly, fried in pumpkin-spiced batter with gravy for dipping—it was absurdly good.

Bay Area Microbreweries

Tampa Bay makes world-class beer. Arguably the best known micro-brewery in the Bay Area (and all of Florida for that matter) is Cigar City Brewing. Opened in 2009 by Joey Redner and Brewmaster Wayne Wambles, Cigar City Brewing's beer quickly got the attention of critics and connoisseurs across the nation. Many believe this was the spark that ignited the now burgeoning craft beer scene in the Tampa Bay area, and concordantly has begun Tampa's transition from a wimpy "fizzy yellow beer" town to a city drinking high-quality locally brewed ales. Check out one of the gems on this list for the finest suds we have to offer.

Barley Mow, 518 W. Bay Dr., Largo, FL 33770; (727) 584-7772; barleymowbrewingco.com. Another great example of a couple who successfully chased their dream of opening a brewery, Jay Dingman and Colleen Huffman were two avid homebrewers who took their passion and turned it into a business. A barley mow literally refers to a stack of barley that was often used to make beer, although it is also the name of a popular English/Irish/Scottish drinking song over 150 years old. The city of Largo, sandwiched in between Clearwater and St. Petersburg, has never been known as a craft beer destination, but Jay and Colleen intend to change that. Their nano-brewery is also a craft beer bar, and the profits from sales of local and national microbrews helped fund getting their own brewery up and running, producing their own recipes, and exploring their addition to the Bay's craft beer scene.

Cigar City Brewing, 3924 W. Spruce St., Tampa, FL 33607; (813) 348-6363; cigarcitybrewing.com. The shining jewel in Tampa's craft brew crown, Cigar City Brewing put Florida on the map as a state with world-class beer in 2009. The first question most people ask (who haven't yet visited the brewery) is "Isn't that in Ybor?" This is an easy mistake to make, as historic Ybor City has numerous old cigar factories, cigar shops, and other cigar-related businesses, but Cigar City Brewing has always resided on Spruce Street, behind the Home Depot just north of Highway 275 on Dale Mabry Highway. The beer is really something impressive. Owner Joey Redner and Brewmaster Wayne Wambles set out to make beers that were really "big" (meaning they have complex layers of flavors and aromas, and a substantial body), and that is exactly what they accomplished. Shortly after releasing their Hunahpu's Imperial Stout (brewed with raw cacao nibs, ancho and pasilla chiles, and vanilla bean), the brew shot to the top of the international rating charts on beer enthusiast websites and caused quite a stir in the industry. Their first year at the Great American Beer Festival in Denver, Colorado, the brewery took home a gold medal for their cedar wood-aged India Pale Ale, called Jai Alai. After being open for three short years, Cigar City Brewing had increased the number of employees and the volume of beer produced by well over tenfold, and continues to increase to this day. When you're flying in and out of Tampa, if in Tampa International Airport's C Terminal, CCB beer can be had at their nanobrewery, one of the few, if not the only, in the nation where the beer is brewed literally right at the airport. For lovers of craft beer, Cigar City Brewing is not to be missed.

Cold Storage, 4101 N. Florida Ave., Tampa, FL 33603; (813) 374-2101; coldstoragecraftbrewery.com. Brewer of Florida Avenue ales (named for the brewery's location on Florida Avenue just north of Downtown Tampa), Cold Storage produces microbrewed beers that they've intended as easy drinking "gateway" beers for people making the transition from mass-produced big corporate flavorless fizzy beer to real hand-crafted good stuff. Tampa natives Andy, Brent, and Bruce wanted to start a brewery to make beers that drank well in the Florida heat and started with three different brews that do exactly that: Florida Avenue Ale, Florida Avenue Blueberry, and Florida Avenue IPA. Brewery tours are available by appointment and there is no real tasting room to speak of, but many of Tampa's craft beer bars serve Florida Avenue beers, so they won't be hard for visitors to find.

Dunedin Brewery, 937 Douglas Ave., Dunedin, FL 34698; (727) 736-0606; dunedinbrewery.com. Dunedin is a small city in northern Pinellas County that has a great community feel and friendly residents. It is also home to Florida's oldest microbrewery. Dunedin Brewery is also a brewpub, with a menu of pub favorites for happy patrons to munch on while enjoying their delicious hand-crafted brews. Dunedin's standard year-round lineup includes an Apricot Peach Ale (their most popular), a Wheat, a Red, a Gold, a Pale, a Brown, and a Nitro Stout. The year-rounders are pretty tasty and easy-drinking, but the limited-release brews are where things really get fun, such as the Bière de Cafe, an American brown ale brewed with locally roasted coffee, or The Rock, Dunedin's big, bold double IPA with intense hoppy character and aroma. The brewery is a fun space to explore, with a separate bar tucked away in a side room, and the main space decorated with large hanging Scottish flags and kilts (Dunedin was settled by Scottish families in the nineteenth century). Live music is common, and the space makes an excellent venue for get-togethers but is just as conducive to relaxing and enjoying a complex creation on a sunny Florida day. Many of Dunedin's limited-release beers achieve an alcohol content as high as 7 or 8 percent, so be sure to enjoy them in moderation!

Peg's Cantina, 3038 Beach Blvd., Gulfport, FL 33707; (727) 328-2720; pegscantina.com. Nestled in cozy Gulfport, Florida, Peg's Cantina is the neighborhood place to be for good food and great beer. Owners Peg and Tony met at Tampa's University of South Florida while both earning PhDs, fell in love, and after graduating moved to New York to be professors. A few years passed and they both greatly missed sunny Florida, so they decided to move back and give up teaching in favor of following their dream of opening a restaurant. Peg and Tony renovated a bungalow in Gulfport, added brewing equipment and a full kitchen, and Peg's Cantina was born. Peg's very talented son Doug brews beers at the restaurant (which, of course, makes it a brewpub) and also has served as assistant brewmaster at Cigar City Brewing. Doug's brews (called G.O.O.D. beers, for Gulfport Original On Draft) have won multiple awards locally and beyond, and a couple even sit on the "top 100 beers in the world" list on beer enthusiast websites. Peg's menu is Mexican fusion, with yummy burritos, quesadillas, tacos, and even pizzas on it, and it serves as a perfect complement to the excellent brews. In addition Peg's has a fantastic outdoor porch and garden seating

Rapp Brewing, 10930 Endeavour Way, Seminole, FL, 33777; (727) 692-7912; rappbrewing.com. Greg Rapp is a beloved beer enthusiast who went from amateur homebrewer to pro homebrewer, won numerous awards for his beers, founded the Pinellas County Urban Brewers Guild (a group of fellow homebrewing enthusiasts that quickly grew to over 100 members), and finally, bought a space and built a brewery. Greg bought a 3,200-square-foot warehouse in Pinellas Park and converted 650 square feet of that into a tasting room; the rest will be used to house brewing equipment and supplies. Greg plans to brew big and exciting beers, continuing to explore his talent and expand his abilities, adding a new beer destination for microbrew aficionados visiting the Bay area, and a new neighborhood spot for Pinellas County residents to frequent and support.

Saint Somewhere Brewing, 1441 Savannah Ave., Tarpon Springs, FL 34689; (813) 503-6181; saintsomewherebrewing.com. Bob Sylvester was an avid homebrewer until people finally convinced him he needed to commercially brew and bottle his beer so it could be shared with everyone, and he did. At first Bob would brew his Belgian-style ales using high-quality ingredients in the traditional open-fermentation style, and bottle with the help of friends and fans (who were paid in rations of beer, of course) until he was finally able to turn his dream and hobby into his full-time occupation. Saint Somewhere beers can now be found in stores as far away as New York City and farther, and they continue to grow in popularity every week. Distribution that far away from home is pretty impressive for such a small operation! Although Bob would probably be happy to show you around his brewery, scheduled guided tours aren't really the norm, so call ahead if you plan to stop by and see the facility.

Seventh Sun, 1012 Broadway, Dunedin, FL 34698; (727) 733-3013; seventhsunbrewing.com. Veteran brewers and boyfriend-and-girlfriend team Justin Stange (formerly of local Cigar City Brewing and Atlanta's Sweetwater Brewery) and Devon Kreps (also formerly of Sweetwater Brewery) started officially pouring beer at their tiny Dunedin brewery January 7, 2012. Hundreds of fans from all over Tampa Bay came out in support and celebration of the great new brewery, congratulating Justin and Devon for getting past the endless hurdles involved in opening a brewery in the Bay area (which is ten times more difficult than most people think). Seventh Sun's brews are huge, dynamic, exciting, and unique. Some of the best known are the FYA, a single-hopped extra pale ale, and the Midnight Moonlight, a fantastic and slightly tart Berliner Weisse. All of Seventh Sun's brews are fantastic, although people just getting into craft beer should be ready for the bold flavors in many of the beers—they're brewed with beer fanatics in mind, and beer fanatics crave big flavor!

Tampa Bay Brewing Company, 1600 E. 8th Ave., Tampa, FL 33605; (813) 247-1422; tampabaybrewingcompany.com. Located in the center of Tampa's historic Ybor City district (cleverly titled "Centro Ybor"), Tampa Bay Brewing Company has been serving up delicious brews and tasty grub at their newer location since 2006. Originally founded in 1996 by the Doble family, TBBC outgrew its original 15th Street home in favor of the new brewpub, which also has fantastic outdoor patio seating and a shaded outdoor bar to boot. The Doble family still operates the brewpub, with Vicki Doble acting as general manager and Dave Doble as brewmaster. TBBC's signature beer is the Old Elephant Foot IPA, a highly hopped India Pale Ale registering around 7 percent ABV and 80 IBUs, a very fragrant, strong IPA perfect for "hop-heads." If an ultra-hoppy beer doesn't sound enticing, worry not; Tampa Bay Brewing

Company also makes a Blonde, an Amber, a Porter, a Weizen, a Stout, and even a Barleywine! Seasonal and experimental beers are constantly being brewed, so on any given day something unique and interesting will be available at the brewpub. Dining at TBBC is as fun as drinking, the creative menu and daily specials are well complemented by the house beers, and to simplify pairing a tasty brew with your meal, the staff prints recommended pairings under the entrees. Although the whole menu is pretty solid, burgers are usually a sure thing at the brewpub, such as the Brewer's Choice Burger, topped with a small mound of blue cheese and a stack of black and tan onion rings, or The "Bomb" (a half-pound burger topped with bacon, cheddar, fries, and onion rings, then wrapped in pizza dough and baked, with a side of horseradish ale sauce). Chances are good you won't leave Tampa Bay Brewing Company hungry or thirsty!

Food Lovers' Itinerary

Are you visiting Tampa with only a day to explore? Here is a sample itinerary not for the faint of stomach that showcases quite a bit of the city's flavor. Too much to chew on? Breaking this tour into two days (schedule allowing) and trying additional goodies at each spot makes for a much more relaxed adventure.

Just a day in Tampa. Let's make it a great day. Assuming today isn't a Sunday (if it is, just disregard all this and go eat until you explode at **Oystercatchers**'s amazing brunch (p. 107), start out with an artfully roasted and hand-crafted coffee creation at **Buddy Brew Coffee** (p. 37) and have a chat with the friendly and knowledgeable baristas about any fun events that may be going on for the day. Breakfast lovers should check out the pancake sandwich or stuffed Cuban bread french toast at **Pinky's** (p. 26), or if today happens to be a weekend day, the devilishly good red velvet pancakes at **Datz** (p. 15) with cream cheese icing taste as great as they look.

Lunch brings us inevitably to **Pane Rustica** (p. 25). Show up early-ish (it gets pretty packed by noon), grab the daily specials menu, and order to your heart's content. The southern half of the restaurant is table service, the northern half is less formally so, although neither half is really "formal-formal" (remember, this is Florida). Sandwiches come on fresh baked in-house bread, and the day's unique pizza creations are fantastically crispy and topped with whatever the chefs have fresh and feel like designing at the moment. Entrees are well thought out and equally well seasoned, but they can be filling so make sure you behave because there is still a lot more eating to do . . .

A mid-afternoon snack is in order, as you only have one day and need to try as much as possible! Swing by **The Floridian** (p. 19), where you can get a 5-inch Cuban sandwich combo with their Floridian bean soup, a great showing of Tampa's official sandwich that is reasonably sized and will leave some room for the rest of the day's adventure. Remember, no lettuce or tomato on that Cuban— you'll compromise the integrity of the sandwich and risk looking like a tourist!

Given that you're only minutes away, now would be a fantastic time to go check out **Cigar City Brewing** (p. 203) and try a pint of sweet, delicious nectar from one of the country's top microbreweries! Take a tour and see what has quickly grown from a two-man operation to a buzzing brewery, working all hours to keep up with the local, national, and even international demand for the amazing brews.

Ybor City

There is no more culturally significant historic area of Tampa than Ybor City. After his cigar factory burned down in Cuba, Vincente Martinez Ybor moved his operation a few hundred miles north, to Tampa. In the decades to follow, Ybor would become known for everything from massive cigar production (at one time there were nearly 30 cigar factories employing over 2,000 people hand-making over 150,000 cigars per day) to rampant mafia activity (it's said there are still secret tunnels beneath some buildings that were used to transport booze during Prohibition and other illegal goods) to today's Ybor, which is primarily a nightlife and entertainment district. Even today, some of Ybor's original brick-paved roads are still preserved and in use, as are some of the original buildings, and even some of the original restaurants (The Columbia, etc). College students and other lovers of the nightlife will enjoy Ybor's many nightclubs, and eateries stay open late so bar-hoppers can soak up some of the drinks they've had with a Cuban sandwich or slice of pizza. A caution: If you are visiting Tampa or unfamiliar with the area, be sure not to venture too far away from Ybor's main strip, as some of the surrounding areas can get a bit sketchy at times.

If you need a moment to walk off some of that delicious grub, go take a stroll through historic Ybor City and see buildings, streets, and monuments that date back into the 1800s. If you've managed to work up a small appetite, the century-old Tampa staple **Columbia** restaurant (p. 61) also makes a great Cuban sandwich and has an absolutely gorgeous interior worthy of exploration even if you aren't hungry. If a cool and refreshing adult beverage is what the doctor ordered, their sangria is well worth a taste, too!

As afternoon approaches evening, a casual stroll or relaxing drive down South Tampa's Bayshore Boulevard is a great way to enjoy some beautiful homes, both classic and modern, on Tampa's well-to-do drive with a view. Home to one of the longest continuous waterfront sidewalks in the nation, Bayshore Boulevard is a very popular spot for runners and cyclists of all ages to get out and exercise with a heck of a view, and it also fortunately puts you the eater within minutes of your next destination on your food adventure . . .

Don some business-casual clothes and head up to **Sidebern's** (p. 28) bar area for the best happy hour in Tampa; just make sure to get there before 7 p.m.! An ever-evolving menu of seasonal, fresh, locally sourced fare, artfully concocted and plated, is served by some of the most fantastic servers and bartenders the Bay has to offer. Artisan cocktails with the highest-quality small-batch liquors and mixers in a downright modern-sexy space, an equally beautiful menu, and an amazing staff—it's no question that much of Tampa Bay considers Sidebern's to be the best restaurant around.

One last bite? A quick phone call for dessert reservations and then head 400 paces due south to the world-famous **Bern's Steakhouse** (p. 34), up a flight of stairs, and voila! You're in the Harry Waugh dessert room. You'll experience a whole new flavor of classic-sexy, seated inside an enormous wine cask that has been converted into a private booth while choosing piped-in music tableside and ordering from the most impressively comprehensive list of spirits by the glass in Tampa. All the desserts are decadent and fantastic, but veterans of this Tampa institution will tell you the King Midas (carrot cake with macadamia nut ice cream) is the can't-miss menu item. The same veterans may tell you of an off-menu secret that exists only when dining in the bar . . . a steak sandwich or hamburger made with the trimmings of some of Tampa's finest cuts of beef . . . but if you ate that, then what would you save for your next visit?

Recipes

Chef Xuan Hurt
of Stinky Bunz Food Truck

Xuan Hurt has an infectiously lovable personality, and it shows in her food, too. Xuan (pronounced "Sing") is of Vietnamese descent and was former owner of a local Vietnamese restaurant prior to starting Stinky Bunz Food Truck with husband Kevin Hurt. Today Xuan shares her love of Asian food with the citizens of Tampa Bay, a welcome addition to the food scene! For more on Stinky Bunz Food Truck see p. 197.

Lemongrass Pork Patties

Yields 28 servings (28 small patties)

- 1 tablespoon fish sauce
- 1 tablespoon sugar
- 1 tablespoon vegetable oil
- 1 small shallot, finely chopped
- 1 small clove garlic, finely chopped

- 2 tablespoons lemongrass, finely chopped (I buy frozen and let thaw in fridge)
- Freshly ground black pepper to taste
- 2 pounds ground pork

In a bowl, whisk together fish sauce and sugar until the sugar is completely dissolved. Add oil, shallot, garlic, lemongrass, pepper, and ground pork, and mix until well combined. Shape into round patties.

Grill or panfry the patties, turning the pieces frequently to prevent burning, until medium-well done, about 10 minutes. Transfer pork patties to a serving dish.

Cucumber Kimchi

Yields 2 servings (2 cups)

- 1 pound pickle cucumbers (may use Persian or English)
- 1 teaspoon salt
- 2½ tablespoons sugar
- 1½ tablespoons Korean red chile flakes
- 1½ tablespoons minced fresh ginger
- 4 garlic cloves, minced
- 1 tablespoon fish sauce
- 1 tablespoon gluten-free soy sauce
- 1 scallion, thinly chopped

Using mandoline or by hand, thinly slice cucumbers. In a bowl, toss the cucumbers with salt and let stand for 10 minutes. Rinse with water and drain.

In a separate bowl, mix the sugar with the chile flakes, ginger, garlic, fish sauce, and soy sauce. Toss in the scallion and cucumbers and coat evenly. Refrigerate. Enjoy!

Fresh Apple Slaw

Yields 28 servings (7 quarts)

Slaw

2 Fuji apples, cores removed, then julienned with skin on

1 small napa cabbage, finely sliced

1 small jicama, peel removed, then julienned

Dressing

2 lemons, zest and juice

3 tablespoons sugar

Splash rice vinegar

½ cup canola oil

Whisk all ingredients together for dressing. Combine slaw and dressing. Refrigerate and enjoy!

Recipes Courtesy of Chef Xuan Hurt

Chef Gary Moran of Wimauma

Gary Moran is no stranger to cooking. He has knifed at such world-famous establishments as Le Bernadin, Bouley, and Tavern on the Green in New York City, but he is a Tampa native (as is his wife) and decided to bring his talents back to Tampa to expand the culinary scene here with his upscale Modern Southern Cuisine. Gary's restaurant Wimauma bears the creedo "Fresh. Local. Florida." and his (locally sourced, Floridian inspired) food exemplifies exactly that. For more on Wimauma see p. 33.

Black Pepper Gravy

Yields 20 servings (2 quarts)

- 1 pound mild country sausage
- ¾ cup flour
- 4½ cups milk
- 1 tablespoon Louisiana-style hot sauce
- 1 tablespoon freshly cracked black pepper
- Salt to taste
- 2 tablespoons butter

In a large high-sided sauce pan (Windsor Pan), cook sausage over medium-high heat until browned and crumbly. Reduce heat to medium and add flour to sausage; mix thoroughly. Cook until flour browns, about 4 minutes stirring constantly (roux brune). Add milk slowly and increase heat to medium-high. Continue to stir. Add hot sauce, pepper, and salt. As the gravy comes to a boil, it will thicken. If too thick, add additional milk. After boiling for 2 minutes, reduce heat to a simmer and add butter. Taste the gravy—it should be smooth, velvety, porky, and finish with a sharp black pepper kick.

Collard Greens

Yields 12 servings (1 gallon)

2 pounds rough chopped bacon ends and pieces (country ham makes an excellent substitute; I like Benton's)

1 cup canola oil

4 Spanish onions, cut into fine julienne

12 cloves garlic, finely minced

4 large bunches collards, stripped from tough central stem and cut into 1½-inch pieces

1 gallon chicken or pork stock, or water

2 cups red wine vinegar

1 tablespoon crushed red pepper

½ cup sugar

In a large stockpot, sweat the chopped bacon in oil until it begins to color a nice golden brown. Add sliced onions and garlic and sweat until they begin to soften. Add the collards and deglaze with the stock or water. Add red wine vinegar, crushed red pepper, and sugar. Lower the temperature of the pot and allow the collards to simmer slowly. Be sure to check that the greens are not adhering to the bottom of the pot, as even a small amount of burn will ruin the whole batch. Cook partially covered for 2½ to 3 hours, or until the greens have turned a drab army green. It is best to let them sit a day before serving, as the flavors continue to blend and develop.

Crispy Fried Florida Oysters with Guacamole, Cilantro & Smoked Tomato Jam

Yields 6 servings

Smoked Tomato Jam

6 Florida beefsteak tomatoes, blanched, shocked, peeled, and rough chopped

1 cup sugar

2 tablespoons water

1 garlic clove, finely minced

1 teaspoon crushed red pepper

½ cup sherry vinegar

Guacamole

2 Haas avocados

1 Roma tomato, quartered, seeded, and small diced (concassé)

½ small red onion, finely minced

2 jalapeños, seeded and small diced

2 limes, juice and zest

1 garlic clove, finely minced

1 teaspoon ground cumin

1 small bunch cilantro, finely chopped

A few dashes Crystal or Tabasco hot sauce

Salt and pepper, to taste

Mix guacamole ingredients to combine.

Smoke the tomatoes for 45 minutes at 200°F in a hard wood smoker (Florida oak is best). Combine the sugar and water and make a medium-gold caramel. Add remaining ingredients and cook in caramel for 25 minutes, or until mixture becomes thick and tacky (be careful when you add the cold ingredients to the hot

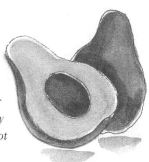

caramel; it will splatter and spit). Puree in blender and place in squeeze bottle when cool.

Fried Florida Oysters

24 Florida oysters, shucked (I prefer Apalachicola)

Drain off all oyster liquid and soak the oysters in buttermilk for at least 1 hour. Dredge oysters in your favorite fry flour recipe and hold until you are ready to serve (it is a good idea to do this the day before, so that the oysters will saturate the fry flour and therefore adhere better to the cracker meal, ensuring a perfectly crispy oyster). When ready to serve, dredge oysters in fine cracker meal and fry in deep fat fryer at 375°F for 3 minutes, or until oysters are a dark golden brown.

To Serve—

Place 4 small football-shaped dollops of guacamole (quenelle) on a round plate in a radial design (a sunburst).

Place an oyster on each quenelle and squeeze a small dollop of the smoked tomato jam on each oyster. Place a third of a cilantro leaf directly on top of the smoked tomato jam and serve with a garnish of torn watercress leaves placed in the middle of the plate.

Jalapeño-Cheddar Spoonbread

Yields 8 servings

4 cups milk
1⅓ cups yellow cornmeal
2 teaspoons kosher salt
4 cups shredded cheddar cheese, divided

1 cup canned corn kernels, drained
½ cup finely diced jalapeño
8 large eggs, lightly beaten
½ cup butter, cut in small pieces

Preheat oven to 400°F.

In a medium saucepan, whisk together the milk, cornmeal, and salt. Cook over medium-high heat, stirring constantly, until mixture has thickened, about 5 minutes. Stir in 2 cups cheese, the corn, and ¾ of the jalapeño. Temper the eggs by slowly whisking some of the hot milk mixture into the beaten eggs. Stir the tempered eggs into the milk mixture. Portion the mixture into 4-ounce ramekins. Top with pieces of butter and sprinkle with the remaining cheese and jalapeño. Bake for 25 to 30 minutes or until center is set and cheese is lightly browned.

Pickled Peaches

Yields 8 servings (2 quarts)

12 pounds small, firm peaches	**4 sticks cinnamon**
6 pounds sugar	**2 tablespoons cloves**
6 cups cider vinegar	**1 large thumb ginger, brunios**

Blanch and shock the peaches to loosen skin. The time is variable because if the peaches are under-ripe this will take considerably longer. Peel peaches, cut in half, and remove the stones.

Combine the sugar, cider vinegar, cinnamon, cloves, and ginger and bring to a simmer (place the cinnamon and cloves in cheesecloth if you are worried about

extracting them). Bring to boil and allow to simmer for about 30 minutes, to concentrate the syrup (it is ready when it is a rich nut brown). Add peaches and simmer in syrup for 6 to 8 minutes. Allow peaches to cool in syrup. You could can them at this point, or just store in fridge until ready to use. The syrup is great as a sauce as well. Reduce to half original volume and add bourbon in the last 15 minutes of reduction to create a tart and mellifluous sauce for desserts or grilled pork.

Recipes Courtesy of Chef Gary Moran

Chef Heather Ann Stalker of Datz

Datz Gastropub in South Tampa employs numerous chefs, one of the most interesting of whom is their "Jill of all Trades," Heather Stalker. Heather is a CIA graduate and one of the more creative young food minds in Tampa, bringing elegance to comfort food, and vice versa. The recipes below show a sample of what dishes at Datz may be like—comfort food, elevated. For more on Datz see p. 15.

Datz Eberson's Old Fashioned

Serves 4–6

- 3 Luxardo cherries
- 0.5 ounce lemon juice
- 1 sugar cube
- 2 dashes Fee Brothers cherry bitters

- 2 ounces Buffalo Trace bourbon
- 1 ounce Dolin sweet vermouth
- Fever Tree club soda
- Candied Bacon skewer for garnish

In a rocks glass (NOT a mixing glass), muddle the cherries with the lemon juice, sugar cube, and the bitters. Add the bourbon, sweet vermouth, and ice. Stir to combine. Top with a float of club soda and the skewer of candied bacon.

Candied Bacon

- 1 pound thickly sliced center-cut bacon
- 1 tablespoon black pepper to taste

- ¼ cup brown sugar
- Bamboo skewers (small)

Preheat oven to 325°F.

Put bacon slices in a bowl, season them with pepper, and toss with the brown sugar. Cover a baking sheet with parchment or foil and arrange the bacon in a single layer on top. Sprinkle any sugar left in the bowl over the bacon. Place the tray in the center of the oven and bake for 20 minutes. Check the bacon often. If it is not golden brown and fairly crispy, resist the temptation to turn up the oven temperature, and cook it for 10 to 15 minutes longer. Check it again. When it's ready, remove from the oven, cool slightly, and then thread onto bamboo skewers.

Datz Bacon Mac n' Cheese

Serves 4–6

1 pound uncooked elbow
   macaroni
½ stick butter
1½ cups evaporated milk
2 cups cubed sharp cheddar
   cheese
½ cup cubed smoked Gouda

½ cup cubed fontina
16 ounces Velveeta
¼ cup diced jalapeño
¼ cup diced Nueske's bacon
Sheet pan
Plastic wrap
Panko bread crumbs

In a large stockpot, bring salted water to a boil and cook the macaroni for 1 minute less than the directions say on the box. Drain, but do NOT rinse.

Return the pasta to the pot, add butter, milk, and cheeses, and mix well until the cheese is melted and fully incorporated. Add the jalapeño and bacon, then mix again.

Pour the macaroni mixture onto a sheet pan lined with plastic wrap, spreading it out evenly. Put the pan in the fridge for 5 to 10 minutes to cool.**

At this point, you can either divide the mixture into dinner-size portions and refrigerate, or you can serve. To serve, put the mac in a heat-proof dish (we like cast iron!), sprinkle panko bread crumbs liberally on top, and put the mixture under the broiler for 2 minutes until golden brown and bubbling!

** If you are interested in making Barry C's Mac n' Cheese Stuffed Meat Loaf, as featured on the Travel Channel's Food Paradise, *stop the process here and see below!*

Barry C's Mac n' Cheese Stuffed Meat Loaf

Serves 4–6

1 portion Datz Bacon Mac n'
   Cheese
3 eggs
2 tablespoons yellow mustard
½ cup ketchup
½ cup diced green peppers

½ cup diced yellow onion
2½ pounds 80 percent lean
   ground chuck
1½ teaspoon salt
1½ teaspoon pepper
½ cup crushed saltine crackers

Take your cooled Datz Bacon Mac n' Cheese mixture (see above), and roll it in plastic wrap, forming a tight log just smaller than your meat loaf pan (approximately 8 inches). Wrap the log in another sheet of plastic, firmly twisting the ends to seal and place in the freezer until hard (approximately 2 hours).

Meanwhile, in a large bowl, combine eggs, mustard, ketchup, green peppers, and onion together, then add the ground beef. Mix lightly, then fold in the salt, pepper, and crushed crackers. Knead the mixture together until fully incorporated.

To stuff and finish: preheat oven to 375°F.

Cover a large cutting board with plastic wrap. Scoop the meat mixture on to the plastic wrap. Pat it out to form a rectangle covering the board about ¾ inch thick.

Remove the mac n' cheese log from the freezer and peel off the plastic wrap. Place the log in the center of the meat loaf, lengthwise, and then wrap the meat around the mac n' cheese, so that the mac is completely covered. Place the mixture into a loaf pan, removing all plastic wrap, and pat the meat until it is smooth and fills the pan.

Bake for an hour, or until fully browned. Let rest for 10–15 minutes before serving. Glaze with more ketchup, then slice and enjoy.

Poutine

If french fries smothered in a demi-glace gravy and topped off with cheese sounds like a plate of heaven to you, then you'll love this take on the Canadian favorite . . . with an egg!

Serves 4–6

Peanut oil

3 cups (approx. 24 ounces) french fries, frozen, skin on

4.5 cups demi-glace or brown gravy

6 large eggs

2 cups cheddar cheese curds

Note: You can find demi-glace or cheese curds at many fine gourmet food stores.

Preheat the oil in a fryer or deep cast-iron pan to 350°F. Fry the skin-on french fries until golden brown, approximately 6 minutes. (For a crispier fry, fry once for 4 minutes at 300°F, cool, then fry again for another 4 minutes at 350°F.)

Remove and drain on paper towels. Season with salt and pepper.

Meanwhile, heat the prepared demi-glace or brown gravy in a saucepan and keep warm.

Lastly, place a large nonstick skillet over medium-high heat and cook the eggs over easy, being sure to keep the yolks runny.

In a bowl, layer as follows: fries, cheese, gravy, and then 1 or 2 eggs.

Season to taste with freshly ground black pepper and kosher salt.

Pastrami Pork Belly

Serves 4–6

¼ cup coriander seed
¼ cup black peppercorns
1 tablespoon allspice
5 pounds Berkshire pork belly
2 cups rice vinegar
1 cup sugar

6 ounces mustard seeds
1 loaf pumpernickel
Fresh sauerkraut
1 jar Russian or 1,000 Island dressing (your favorite)
5 ounces Parmigiana Reggiano

In a small sauté pan over medium heat, toast the coriander, peppercorns, and allspice. Cool, then grind in a spice grinder. Coat the pork belly with the toasted spice mixture and place into a smoker at 220°F for 2 hours.

Preheat oven to 375°F. Once the pork belly has been smoked, transfer it to the oven and let it cook for an additional 2 hours. Then, let cool for at least 2 hours or overnight. Slice pork belly into 1-inch-thick slabs, then cut again into 2-inch-thick cubes.

To pickle mustard seeds: Combine vinegar and sugar in a saucepan, and bring to a boil. Add mustard seeds and turn off heat. Let sit.

To serve: Gently reheat pastrami pork belly in a 250°F oven or toaster oven. Toast the pumpernickel bread and cut diagonally into small toast points (aka crostini). Set aside.

To plate: Place sauerkraut on a plate. Add a dollop of dressing. Then pumpernickel bread. Finish with pork belly. Garnish with pickled mustard seeds and shaved Parmigiana Reggiano.

Recipes Courtesy of Chef Heather Ann Stalker

Chef Chad Johnson of Sidebern's

Chad Johnson took an already excellent restaurant in Sidebern's and took it a step further. Committed to using locally sourced ingredients whenever possible, his continuously changing menus are unforgivingly exploratory, enticing, and elegant all at the same time. Chad's menu (as you will see in the recipes below) are dynamic, inventive, and exciting, and should impress anyone you choose to prepare them for! For more on Sidebern's see p. 28.

Roasted Gulf Shrimp with Aleppo Pepper, Lime, & Miso Mayonnaise

Yields 8 servings

16 giant shelled, head-on shrimp

Aleppo Pepper Glaze

1 tablespoon minced garlic
1 tablespoon Aleppo pepper
Olive oil (enough to coat bottom of pan)
1 cup white wine
Zest of 2 limes (for garnish)

½ cup chopped sun-dried tomatoes
½ cup lime juice
1 ounce sherry vinegar
2 ounces lime juice

Sweat garlic and Aleppo pepper in olive oil until fragrant.

Add wine and reduce by half.

Add remaining ingredients and simmer for 10 minutes.

Puree, strain through a fine mesh sieve.

Miso Mayonnaise

3 ounces miso

2 ounces Dijon mustard

1 egg yolk

1 cup extra-virgin olive oil

1 ounce lime juice

Mix miso, Dijon, and egg in a bowl.

Emulsify olive oil by slowly whisking into the miso mixture.

Season with lime juice.

Assembly

Roast shrimp in olive oil over medium-high heat

When shrimp are 80 percent cooked, remove from the pan and lightly brush with the pepper glaze.

Return shrimp to the pan and continue cooking until the glaze is caramelized.

Spoon miso mayonnaise in the center of a plate.

Place glazed shrimp on the mayonnaise and garnish with grated lime zest.

BBQ Ceviche

Yields 12 servings

- 2 tablespoons extra-virgin olive oil
- 1 cup minced red bell peppers
- 2 tablespoons chopped garlic
- ½ cup minced fennel
- ½ cup minced celery
- 2 cups lime juice
- 1½ cups orange juice
- 1 cup sherry vinegar
- ¾ cup Worcestershire sauce
- ¼ cup molasses
- ¼ cup honey
- ¼ cup whole grain mustard
- 1 cup ketchup
- 2 tablespoons ancho chile powder
- 2 tablespoons ground coriander seed
- 3 tablespoons ground cumin
- 1 tablespoon smoked paprika
- 2 pounds fresh fish or shellfish cut into 1-inch cubes

Place olive oil, bell peppers, garlic, fennel, and celery in a stainless steel pan and cook over low heat until the vegetables begin to turn translucent.

Add all remaining ingredients except the seafood to the pan and slowly bring to a simmer.

Once the mixture has been brought to a simmer, transfer to a clean pan and cool over ice.

Add the diced seafood to the cooled ceviche base. Allow the seafood to marinate under refrigeration for 12 hours before serving.

Garnish with tortilla chips or salted popcorn.

Roasted Asparagus with Quail Egg, Sorrel, Black Truffle Fonduta

Serves 4

2 ounces heavy cream
1 cup taleggio cheese
Zest of 1 lemon
1 tablespoon black truffle oil
20 spears asparagus

12 poached quail eggs
1 ounce grated Parmesan cheese
24 sorrel leaves
Shaved black truffles (optional)

Place heavy cream and taleggio in a pan over low heat and whisk until smooth in consistency. Add lemon zest, truffle oil, and remove from the heat. Keep warm.

Roast asparagus spears over medium heat in butter until just slightly firm in the center.

Warm pre-poached quail eggs in acidulated water.

For assembly, spoon 2 ounces of the taleggio sauce in the center of the plate. Place roasted asparagus on top of the cheese sauce. Place quail eggs around the asparagus, garnish plate with a dusting of grated Parmesan, sorrel leaves, and shaved black truffles.

Beef Cheek Ravioli with Duck Liver

Yields 4 servings

**8 beef cheek ravioli (recipe
follows)**

**½ cup duck liver sauce (recipe
follows)**

**1 tablespoon BLiS Elixer (high
quality sherry vinegar may
be used as a substitute)**

Boil ravioli for 2 minutes in salted water.

Heat duck liver sauce in sauté pan.

Strain ravioli and put into duck liver sauce; cook 1 additional minute.

Place 2 raviolis on each of 4 plates, spoon liver sauce over top of ravioli.

Garnish with drops of BLiS Elixer.

Beef Cheek Ravioli

Fill pasta sheets (recipe follows) with beef cheek mixture (recipe follows).

Form ravioli, seal edges with egg wash.

Pasta Dough

6 egg yolks
3 cups all-purpose flour

1 tablespoon olive oil

Place oil and eggs in bowl and mix.

Knead flour into egg mixture to form dough.

Allow dough to rest for 1 hour, sheet through pasta roller.

Beef Cheek Filling

5 pounds beef cheeks

2 carrots, chopped

1 onion, chopped

¼ cup olive oil

1 cup sweet sherry

2 cups veal stock

6 bay leaves

2 ounces thyme sprigs

Sear beef cheeks, carrots, and onion in oil.

Deglaze with sherry.

Add remaining items and simmer for 3–4 hours until cheeks are tender.

Once cool, shred beef cheeks.

Duck Liver Sauce

1 tablespoon butter

2 tablespoons finely diced onion

¼ teaspoon ground clove

1 teaspoon cracked black pepper

1 tablespoon chopped sage

½ teaspoon ground cumin

¼ cup sweet sherry

1 tablespoon heavy cream

4 ounces duck liver

Put butter in saucepan and cook until brown.

Add onion and cook until translucent.

Add clove, pepper, sage, and cumin, and sauté for 10 seconds.

Deglaze with sherry, reduce by half.

Add heavy cream and duck liver. Cook until liver is just pink in center.

Puree, pass through a strainer, cool, and reserve.

Recipes Courtesy of Chef Chad Johnson

Chef Andrew Basch of Pelagia Trattoria

Andrew Basch absolutely loves food. Andrew showcases high-quality ingredients in an approachable and creative manner, while lending a bit of whimsical fun (check out the Chocolate "Cigar" and Panna Cotta "Coffee" in the Coffee & Cigars!) to the dishes conceptually. The recipes below can be prepared by home cooks of most experience levels and are sure to delight. For more on Pelagia Trattoria see p. 108.

BBQ Salmon Salad

Yields 2 servings

2 6-ounce salmon portions

Barbecue Rub

4 tablespoons chili powder

2 tablespoons garlic powder

2 tablespoons onion powder

6 tablespoons sugar

1 teaspoon ground cumin

½ teaspoon ground white pepper

2 tablespoons paprika

Combine all ingredients together.

Reserve 3 tablespoons of rub to use for dressing.

Dressing

2 cups pizza sauce

2 tablespoons rice wine vinegar

3 tablespoons barbecue rub

¼ cup olive oil

Put pizza sauce, vinegar, and spice mix in blender.

Slowly add oil.

Salad

1 cup mesclun mix
¼ cup watercress
3 baby beets, cut in half

2 Kumato tomatoes, cut in half
2 tablespoons salad dressing
½ lemon

Mix all ingredients except lemon together.

Squeeze lemon over combined ingredients.

Plate on square.

For the Salmon

Dredge salmon in the barbecue spice rub.

Refrigerate at least 1 hour before grilling.

Spray the salmon portion with cooking spray and place on grill in a medium heat location. Salmon will caramelize due to sugar in the rub, so do not place on hottest section of grill.

Grill salmon, turning halfway through, or until salmon reaches medium temperature.

Place grilled salmon on center of salad mix.

Finish dish with half grilled lemon on the plate.

Jumbo Lump Crab Cakes
with Candied Tomatoes & Tarragon Aioli

Yields 3 servings

1 lemon, zest only
1 lime, zest only
¼ cup tarragon aioli
1 tablespoon panko bread
  crumbs

1 tablespoon fine diced red bell
  pepper
1 pound jumbo lump crab

Combine all ingredients except crab and mix together.

Add crab and gently fold into mixture.

Let chill 1 hour before cooking.

Portion crab cake to desired size, dredge in panko bread crumbs, and sear in hot pan with oil.

Finish in 350°F oven for 5 minutes.

Tarragon Aioli

1 tablespoon Dijon mustard
½ tablespoon capers
2 tablespoons fresh tarragon
½ tablespoon rice vinegar

½ cup mayonnaise
½ teaspoon Old Bay seasoning
½ teaspoon togarashi chili
  (can substitute ¼ teaspoon
  cayenne pepper)

Combine all ingredients in a blender and puree on low until combined.

Candied Tomatoes

3 large tomatoes, peeled and
    seeded
½ cup sugar

¼ cup rice vinegar
½ teaspoon salt

Combine all ingredients in saucepot and simmer, stirring often until tomatoes reach a jam-like consistency. Once most of liquid evaporates, keep a close eye on mixture as it can burn easily at this point.

Presentation: Place tarragon aioli on plate with squeeze bottle or spooned design. Garnish center of plate with tablespoon of candied tomatoes. Rest the seared crab cake in center of plate and garnish with fresh herbs.

Pomegranate Marinated Duck

Yields 4 servings

Marinade

1 cup pomegranate juice
¼ cup grappa
3 tablespoons pomegranate
    molasses

2 sticks thyme
1 shallot, chopped
3 juniper berries

Combine all ingredients to make marinade. Marinate duck skin side up. Do not let marinade cover skin.

Grappa Glaze

1 shallot, diced

¼ cup grappa

1 cup pomegranate juice

2 cinnamon sticks

2 cups demi

Sweat shallots and deglaze with grappa and pomegranate juice. Add cinnamon. Reduce by half. Add demi and cook until nape. Strain.

Polenta

2 cups cream

2 cups water

Salt

8 ounces Italian dry polenta

4 ounces unsalted butter

4 ounces Parmesan cheese

Bring cream, water, and salt to a boil. Whisk in polenta. Cook for 1 hour on low. The polenta will thicken a lot as it cooks. Add water if needed. Finish with butter and cheese.

For the Dish

Put marinated duck into a cold pan and cook to desired temperature. Put polenta in the middle of a round plate with small seasonal vegetables on the right side. Let duck rest and slice it. Put around the front of the plate. Sauce and garnish with pomegranate seeds.

Coffee & Cigars

Yields 4 servings

Espresso Panna Cotta

2 sheets gelatin	**¼ cup granulated sugar**
1½ cups heavy cream	**1 vanilla bean**
½ cup milk	**4 tablespoons espresso**

Bloom gelatin in ice water 5–10 minutes, until soft.

Combine remaining ingredients and bring to simmer, stirring often, for 5 minutes.

Reduce to low and add gelatin.

Cook 5 more minutes or until slightly thickened.

Portion in desired containers and let cool.

Place in refrigerator and let chill at least 4 hours before serving. Will last 2 days.

Chocolate Cigar

1 cup butter	**1 cup all-purpose flour**
1 cup sugar	**1 cup finely ground almonds**
7 ounces corn syrup	**1½ tablespoons cocoa powder**

In mixing bowl cream together butter and sugar.

Slowly add corn syrup until combined.

Add flour and combine.

Add ground almonds and cocoa powder and mix until combined.

Refrigerate at least 1 hour.

On a silicone mat, portion 1 tablespoon of batter and spread to desired shape.

Bake at 320°F until golden.

Allow to cool until you can handle without breaking.

Roll tuile over back of wooden spoon and let cool completely.

Store in airtight container.

For the Dish

Whisk Bailey's into panna cotta base then pipe into cigar.

Fill a cigar and place in the panna cotta then place chocolate shaving at the end of the cigar to look like ash. Place the dish on a baby greens plate with a black napkin under it.

Olive Pâté from Imperia

Yields 5 servings

7 ounces pitted black Kalamata olives

2 ounces fresh butter

½ ounce chopped thyme

Zest of ½ lemon

1 tablespoon extra-virgin olive oil

Black pepper to taste

Pass the olives in the mixer until you have a paste. Add the butter and thyme and mix it again. Add the lemon zest and the olive oil and finish with the black pepper.

Serve with any bread of your choice.

Recipes Courtesy of Chef Andrew Basch

Appendix:
Eateries by Cuisine

Wood Fired Pizza & Wine Bar, 148

Wine Shop
West Palm Wines, 65

Index